D1736517

Gold and Silver in the MOJAVE

Gold and Silver in the
MOJAVE

IMAGES OF A LAST FRONTIER

Nicholas Clapp

SUNBELT PUBLICATIONS
San Diego, California

Gold and Silver in the Mojave: Images of a Last Frontier

Sunbelt Publications, Inc.
Copyright © 2013 by Nicholas Clapp
All rights reserved. First edition 2013, second printing 2015

Book cover and interior design by Lydia D'moch
Project management by Deborah Young
Cartography by Kathleen Wise
Printed in Korea

Sunbelt Publications, Inc.
P.O. Box 191126
San Diego, CA 92159-1126
(619) 258-4911, fax: (619) 258-4916
www.sunbeltbooks.com

18 17 16 15   5 4 3 2

Library of Congress Cataloging-in-Publication Data

Clapp, Nicholas.
Gold and silver in the Mojave : images of the last frontier / Nicholas Clapp.—1st ed.
p. cm.
ISBN 978-0-932653-06-2 (pbk.)
1. Mojave Desert—History—Pictorial works. 2. Mojave Desert—History,
Local—Pictorial works. 3. Frontier and pioneer life—Mojave Desert—Pictorial works.
4. Mining camps—Mojave Desert—History—Pictorial works.
5. Gold mines and mining—Mojave Desert—History—Pictorial works.
6. Silver mines and mining—Mojave Desert—History—Pictorial works.
7. Miners—Mojave Desert—History—Pictorial works.
8. Mojave Desert—Social life and customs--Pictorial works. I. Title.
F868.M65C525 2013
979.4'95—dc23
2013023332

Page i: In a landscape of broken rock, sage and snow, a horse, two miners and a primitive gallows frame have hoisted a bucketful of promising ore—to be examined by four well-dressed men, possibly investors. Would anything come of this? Chances were, yes.
The photograph appears to have been taken in 1902 in the northern Mojave. Not long, and there'd be a settlement here—an explosion of humanity, hope, enterprise, and greed.

Page ii: Eight hundred feet underground, the gold-rich glory hole of a southern Mojave mine.

Dedicated to:

The celebrated and the obscure of the Mojave Desert, 1890–1915.

Prospectors and miners, preachers and harlots,

barkeeps and undertakers, sheriffs and scoundrels.

The land was their home, no matter its repute.

Contents

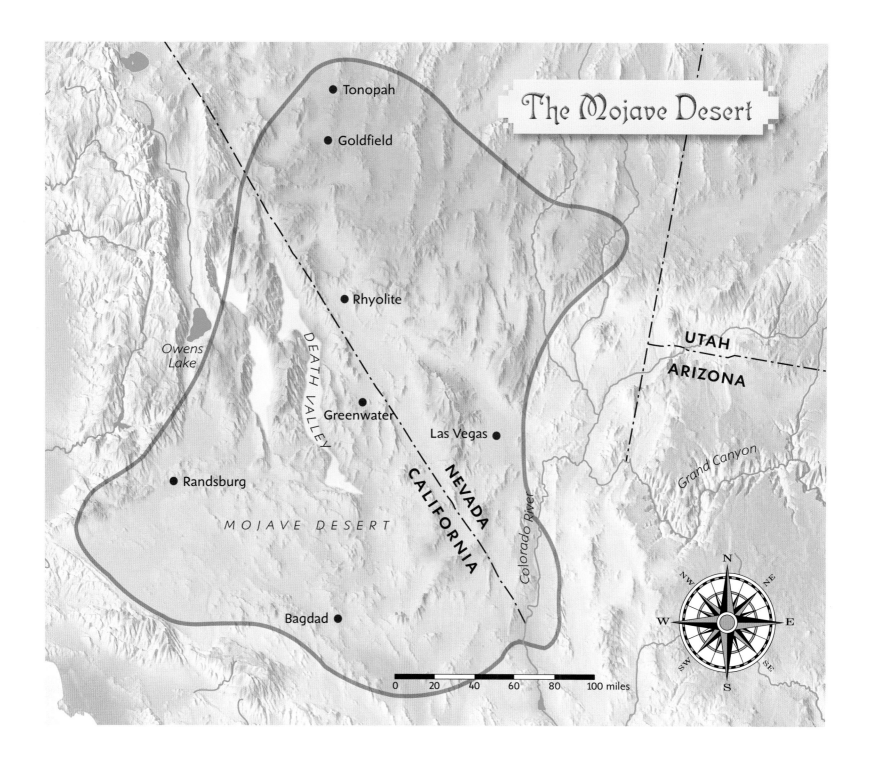

The Mojave Desert

Tonopah

Goldfield

Rhyolite

Owens Lake

DEATH VALLEY

Greenwater

Las Vegas

Randsburg

MOJAVE DESERT

Bagdad

NEVADA
CALIFORNIA

Colorado River

UTAH

ARIZONA

Grand Canyon

N
NW NE
W E
SW SE
S

0   20   40   60   80   100 miles

Prologue

❧━━◦◦━━❧

Historians and geographers are at odds as to what makes the Mojave the Mojave. For good reason, the land was known both as "the land of little rain" and a "country of lost borders."[1]

There were—and still are—Mohave Indians. Was this their tribal land?

Or a geologist might tell you the Mojave is an area bounded by California's San Andreas fault north to the Garlock fault.

Best, perhaps, is a botanical description offered by natural historian Edmund C. Jaeger. He wrote that the Joshua tree was "the Mojave Desert's most distinctive plant. If a line were drawn around this strange tree's distribution, that line pretty well marks out the marginal confines of the Mojave Desert region."

Coincidentally, a century ago, that very line circumscribed a land destined to offer remarkable showings of gold and silver.

Pioneering ladies in a land of little comfort.

1. Phrases to inspire Mary Austin's classic *The Land of Little Rain* (1903) and her later *Lost Borders* (1909).

Gold and Silver in the
MOJAVE

A grizzled prospector on the banks of the Colorado. (An image long misidentified as taken in the '49er foothills of the Sierra Nevada.)

Looks promising.

Gold Along the River

North from the Mexican border to the sleepy rancho of Las Vegas, the serpentine, gently-flowing Colorado offered sands that, if patiently panned, might yield a man a trace of color. In the early 1890s, the river's prospectors were, more often than not, veterans of played-out lodes of the West, with Deadwood, South Dakota, the most recent.

These men and few women were not overly hopeful as to what they might discover.

But then, the muddy waters in their pan would part, and there'd be a nugget. Small, but for its size, heavy.

Gold?

Poke the shiny stuff with a knife; was it brittle or malleable? Spit on it; did it glisten? If brittle and dull, the rock—fool's gold—would, with a mutter of disgust, be chucked over a prospector's shoulder. But if prompting a whoop, the sample would have him tramping dry washes and scrambling peaks in search of more of the same, homing in on its source. Ideally, he would have himself a rich quartz-gold outcropping.

More likely, a showing would be marginal. A little color here and there, but bottoming out at bedrock.

Surveying mining claims west of the Colorado River.

Even so, a coyote hole of ore would be cause for celebration—and an excursion to the saloons and bordellos of Mohave City, Ehrenberg, or Las Vegas.

In these dusty outposts of civilization, a man's poke could be lost to the frock-coated card sharps, the come-hithers of *doves du priarie*, and the attraction and depredation of strong drink.

Then it would be back to the desert and dogged trudging and hammering in the burning sun, with no one to talk to excepting a jackass.

Away from the river, deeper into the Mojave, a fellow could get fidgety, morose, desperate. He could even be tempted to end it all, either slowly with "coffin varnish" whiskey, or quickly with a dose of carbolic acid or *Rough-on-Rats*.

Or . . .

What started as a coyote hole could widen, and if a man had a Pocket Assay Kit, he could get an idea of how many ounces to the ton his vein might yield. If more than an ounce or two (with gold at $32 an ounce), he might just have himself a profitable mine. If four or more ounces, a bonanza!

In a manic rush, a prospector would make an educated guess as to the lay of the vein, and with piles of rock, mark the corners of a 1,500 by 600 foot claim. He would write up what he'd found, and tuck it into a tobacco can wedged in a center-point monument. All the while, he'd nervously scan the surrounding terrain for potential jumpers. He'd then make tracks for the nearest camp recorder or, better yet, county seat. His mind would race . . .

What to name the mine?

Something with heft to it? *The King Solomon, the Imperial*. Or something exotic? *The Zulu Queen, the Silver Witch*. What of a name on the sentimental side? *The Mary Gale, the Valentine* . . .

If a long day got a prospector to the county seat after dark, he'd be at the courthouse door when it opened the next morning. Upon payment of a dollar, a clerk would open a massive leather-bound volume, and in flowing handwriting, describe and date—to the minute (in the event of a rival filing)—the discovery.

Paddy's Pride, the Old Swede. The Gypsy, Yellow Dog, Rose of Peru, Lame Dog, Lost Burro, The Wonder of the World . . .

In Las Vegas, a brace of Knights of the Green Cloth. Note the dangling light bulb. The advent of electricity—and electromagnets—facilitated the rigging of roulette tables.

Just about all there was to Las Vegas prior to the coming of the Southern Pacific Railroad.

Near Willow Springs in the western Mojave, 1893. For morose, downcast E.M. Hamilton a single, shining rock would spell the difference. (Note how, for dramatic effect, the photographer reversed the triumphal image on the facing page.)

In years to come, county clerks from Mohave County, Arizona Territory, over to Inyo County, California, were to blot the ink of hundreds, then thousands of pages of claims.

The Golden Empire, Eastern Star, Storm Jade . . .

The nation might be in an economic malaise, but not here. There was gold, silver too. No certifiable bonanzas yet, but in time and with luck . . .

The Sidewinder, Outlaw, Hidden Hell, Humbug, Great Wanamingo, True Blue, Roulette, Rainbow's End . . .

And what was interesting about all this was that history—or rather, history's exponents—had made no provision for this sound and fury. In 1890, the U.S. Census had declared, "There can hardly be said to be a frontier line." In a speech at Chicago's 1893 Exposition, Harvard's Frederick Jackson Turner lamented "the closing of a great historical movement. . . . The frontier has gone." And with it, the Old West.

But, overlooked, *there was a frontier line*—a looping, irregular line encircling some 50,000 square miles of the Mojave Desert.

In this arid land, unsettled and sketchily mapped—written off as godforsaken and worse—there would now be a headlong twenty-year rush for riches.

And for the Old West: a grand, tumultuous, rowdy Last Act.

A Santa Fe Route promotional booklet.

Randsburg

The Treasure of The Yellow Aster

※——◦◦——※

There was a legendary, fever-inducing lode in the Mojave: the Lost Gunsight. As the name implies, its location was—and remains—uncertain. The story goes that back in '49 a party of misguided emigrants, desperate to escape Death Valley, stumbled on a ledge of silver and from it fashioned a replacement sight for an otherwise useless rifle. The tale—slender at best—was to fire many an imagination, and prompt many an expedition, in the course of which the ledge swelled to a veritable mountain of silver, a mountain that was to wander the Mojave like a restless wraith. It was believed to be off into Nevada; no, it was a day's travel from Barstow and the railroad. The phantom peak offered a generation of prospectors tinseled hope, then rueful despair, then hope anew.

Or, if a man preferred gold to silver, he could pursue the 1864 Lost Breyfogle, named for a prospector who made a strike somewhere up toward Death Valley, but, deranged by sunstroke, could never find his way back.

It was unclear whether droopy-eyed Charles Burcham, toiling as a San Bernadino butcher, was a Gunsighter or Breyfogler (he was said to be both). For certain, he was

Placer mining in the western Mojave. With water scarce, a pair of hand-cranked dry washers part heavier gold from lighter pebbles and dirt. The man to the right examines a riffle that, with luck, glinted with color. Smiling, though, came hard in this "poor man's camp," located up Hard Cash Gulch. Their diggings were within sight of a drab, iron-stained peak to the south. It was little different than any other. Hardly worth prospecting, or so they thought.

Saturday night. Hoping for a better next week than the last.

A determined Dr. Rose La Monte Burcham

smitten by the prospect of precious metal in the Mojave. This increasingly irritated his wife, Rose, a prominent physician, who finally had enough of her husband's feckless dreaming and packed him off to the desert with the promise that she would bankroll a two-year prospecting spree, but that was it. Come up empty-handed, and Charles would be back trimming pork and grinding sirloin.

Burcham's two years were almost up when his wanderings took him to Hard Cash Gulch *(previous page)*, there to partner up with John Singleton, a carpenter, and Frederic Mooers, a hapless journalist. In common, their fortunes were at a low ebb, their pockets empty. Nevertheless, before quitting the country, the trio agreed to join forces for a farewell venture. They would prospect an iron-stained mountain to the south, where the previous year Mooers had noted—and discounted, for they were pitiful—traces of placer gold.

On the day of their departure, there was a matter of sobering Burcham up, and that accomplished, the trio found their way to the peak, and made for its summit. They paused to drink from their canteens and take in the view. Then, as they climbed on, John Singleton lagged behind, to idly knock a specimen from an irregular rock. Turning it over, he "let out a startled exclamation," which had his partners slipping and sliding back down the slope, to shout, "We're rich! By George, Singleton, we've found it! She's a mine, Singleton, right from the grass roots!"[2]

They named the peak *Rand Mountain*, hoping the fortune of the famed South African gold district would rub off on them.

It was Mooers who named their strike. He'd been reading a florid, popular novel in which an aloof, sublimely arrogant, devastating beautiful heroine was likened to a flower that in its rarity and appeal surpassed even the red rose. This, the partners agreed, was a fitting analogy for a lode that defied discovery, yet was now theirs.

The mine would be *The Yellow Aster*.

2. Quoted in Marcia Rittenhouse Wynn, *Desert Bonanza* (Glendale, California: Arthur H. Clark, 1963).

An early road to Randsburg.

A barrel and a plank, and a man had a dining room; two barrels and a plank, a saloon. The fellow to the left is photographer C.W. Tucker. In a three-year desert stay, he created an enduring portrait of the camp's life and seasons.

Beyond the Yellow Aster's boundaries, strikes were made and shafts sunk: The Rustler, Napoleon, Olympus, Blue Rose, White Horse, Gray Eagle, Black Hawk, and a dozen more. The man with the gun, star, and pick may well be sheriff turned miner D.M. Pyle, on record as chaperoning several sacks of high-grade ore to an Oakland smelter.

Uncorking the bottle to celebrate Flag Raising Day at the newly constructed offices of the Yellow Aster Mining & Milling Co. The fourth fellow from the left—in the white suit and straw hat—is the strike's discoverer, Frederick Mooers. His countenance is wan—he would not revel in his fortune; he had taken sick and would soon die.

As best they could, they kept the strike secret. Nevertheless, it wasn't long before the hungry miners across the way in Hard Cash Gulch got wind of the discovery and rushed to the site, only to find the best ground properly staked, recorded, and fiercely guarded by Charles' wife, Dr. Rose La Monte Burcham, up from San Bernardino.

Opposing a quick sale, Dr. Rose was to spurn, with stinging scorn, quick-on-the-scene potential investors. Rather, she believed, she and the three men alone could make a go of it. Thereupon, an arrangement was cobbled to run a first wagonload of Yellow Aster ore through a mill that had fitfully served Hard Cash Gulch. The results were heartening, spectacular even, so much so that the partners feared that a shipment out of the desert would be set upon and hijacked.

While the men pondered what to do, Dr. Rose declared she needed to do some shopping over in the Santa Fe railroad town of Mojave. She suggested that Frederick Mooers accompany her, and once in Mojave, they would arrange for the disposition of the gold. So it was that two passengers and an empty spring wagon jounced away on a dusty track.

Miners and muckers reporting for their shift. They will soon be caked with sweat and rock dust.

On Dr. Rose Burcham's orders, the Yellow Aster was (above ground, at least) an immaculately tended showcase—boasting potted palms, sitting room lighting, and a gold-inlayed flywheel.

13

The ore was declared endless.

The mine was a mix of underground and open pit workings—together a grand glory hole. Early on, a visiting mining engineer advised, "Build a mill and shovel in the Mountain." They did just that in the mill on the ridge to the left.

Mooers handled the team. At his side Dr. Rose chatted on about the scenery, which to her Victorian sensibility was romantically mauve and hazy cerulean blue. Not mean and drab, as most would have it.

And all the while, no one was the wiser that the folds of Dr. Rose's voluminous skirt concealed heavy gold ingots—that would ensure the development of a world beater mine.

Tenderfeet from the East as well as seasoned miners flocked to Randsburg, anxious to be in on the excitement of a wonder camp. More than a few, born to wealth, were out to show their mettle in a still rough-and-tumble West. They'd first try their hand at prospecting, with predictably dismal results. They'd then seek work at a mine like the Yellow Aster, with its payroll approaching 150 men.

Typically, a young man would hire on as a nipper delivering fresh, sharpened steel to drillers, then emptying their thunder jugs. A next step up, and he was a mucker shoveling fractured rock into ore car after ore car. Twelve hour shifts, six days a week. Finally, he might make it as hard-rock miner. Dangerous work—wrestling a "widow maker," an ungainly, thundering pneumatic drill. The pay at the end of this particular rainbow? Just $3.50 a day.

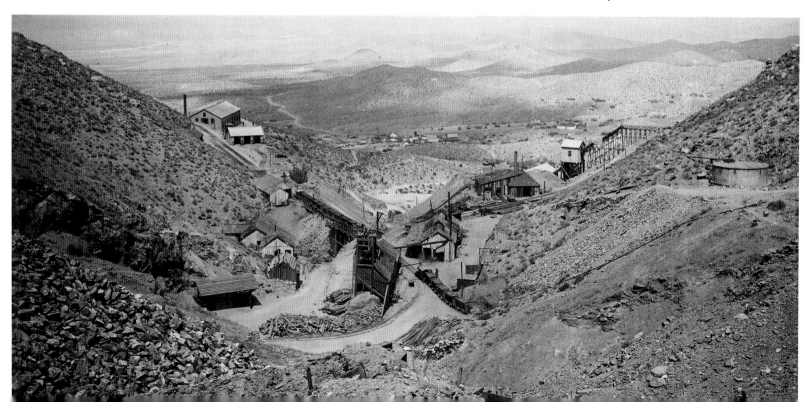

The 100 stamps of the Yellow Aster mill pounded around the clock. Rock was rendered gravel, to spill down 20 mercury-coated copper plates. The mercury would bond with the gold. This amalgam was then roasted to evaporate the mercury—and free the gold. On Dr. Rose's insistence, this normally grimy operation was swept and tidied. Expectorate at your peril! Come nightfall and a somnolent graveyard shift, the operation occasionally lost power, and the thundering of the stamps was suspended. At the foot of the hill, the dead silence would awaken the men, women, and children of sleeping Randsburg.

Randsburg. Winter in the high desert, 1897. One of the handfuls of images stamped on the back: "C.W. Tucker, Pho." Subsequent Mojave photographers would etch their names in the corner of their negatives.

Finishing touches on a hotel that would boast private rooms, indoor plumbing, and hot meals around the clock.

Snow continues to fall. The woman is Grace Tucker, C.W.'s new bride—whisked to Randsburg and schooled in film processing and printing. Samples of C.W.'s work are posted on the door to his tent-studio (to the rear).

Inside Tucker's studio. A system of ropes, pulleys, and overhead canvas flaps directed and enhanced natural light. A closer look reveals his day-in-day-out work to be portraiture—most often to be mailed to family back East.

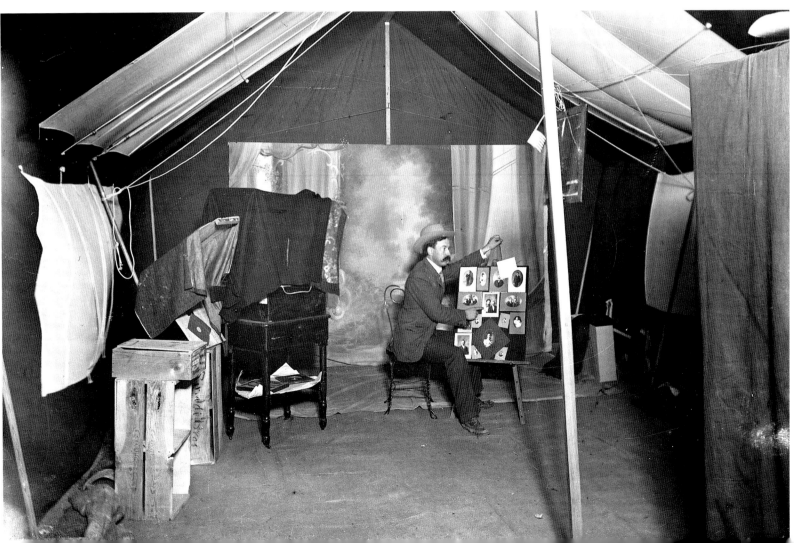

A rare, still moment in a booming camp. Possibly Sunday morning, the one day a week a miner could sleep in.

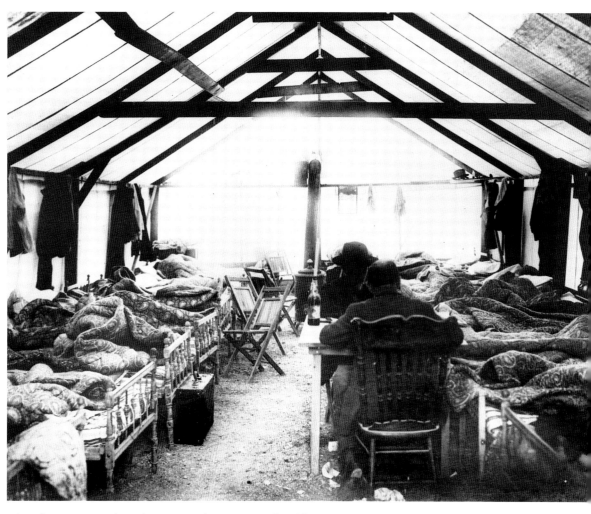

A boarding tent. It's unclear what occupies the two men at the table.
Playing checkers or cribbage? Writing faraway loved ones?

19

Off shift, a miner would wolf down a stew dished up by a "Ma This-or-that," and crave nothing more than sleep. His was a backbreaking, mind-dulling routine, but damned if he would write home asking for a one-way ticket on the Santa Fe, and a return to the arms of Mother and Mary Ann. Then: Enough of feeling sorry for himself! He would hitch up his suspenders, straighten his hat, and head for one or another of Randsburg's Main Street saloons. From personal experience, one Clyde Kuffel wrote,

It was the sound of voices that gave you a lift after being alone, down in a mine shaft all day. The friendship of the bartender, the laughter of the girls, and story swapping with other miners all added up to a pleasant evening that made the day of hard work and uncomfortable living bearable.

In the opposite, evocative photograph of a tent saloon, the girls are missing. It could be that it's midday, and they're asleep. Or, with children present, the photographer may have shooed them off.

The image is engaging in its warmth and humanity . . . of players quietly suspending their game, of the barber hoping for a customer, of the barkeep with his arms around his daughter. Closer, there are details illuminating life in a late nineteenth-century Mojave mining camp.[3]

Randsburg, as early as 1895. The Yellow Aster saloon (with only the name in common with the mine). Pages to follow explore this image.

3. Quoted in Marcia Rittenhouse Wynn, *Desert Bonanza* (Glendale, California: Arthur H. Clark, 1963).

The Bar

Though all else might be coarse or tattered, the bar was often magnificent—in this case a Brunswick crafted in England, shipped round the Horn, and carted from city to town (San Francisco? Bakersfield?) before finding a home in the desert. It would likely move on, to strikes further afield.

Though you can't read the labels, a look at the backbar reveals a handsome assortment of spirits, and below, a neatly-laid stock of wine. A frontier camp's fortune was measured by the quality of its spirits. At the low end—over in Hard Cash Gulch, say—grain alcohol could be flavored with peppers and tobacco juice and passed off as whiskey. At the high end, *Col. Halford's* was in order for toasting Randsburg celebratory occasions, like an unbelievable $20,000 to the ton assay reported for a Yellow Aster stringer. (Not that anyone here present would benefit.) If times were good, wines and champagnes were French. Cocktails, too, could "cut the dust," with Claret Stingarees a camp favorite.[4]

4. 1 1/2 oz. Claret, 1 tsp. powdered sugar, 1 tbsp. brandy.

Here, it might be noted, dubious science had its role in a widespread opinion that *drinking was healthy*, for it preserved—that is to say, pickled—bodily tissues. On the other hand, temperance advocates (though few and far between in the desert) insisted that alcoholic consumption was the *leading cause* of human spontaneous combustion.

Kids

In Randsburg, there was the tale of an adventuresome tyke prone to wander off and become lost in the sagebrush, prompting her mother to outfit her with a sheep bell tied around her neck. Older kids, their lunches in plug tobacco cans, were packed over the hill to school in a more family-oriented, sister camp of Johannesburg. Desert childhoods were fondly recalled. Miner's daughter Marcia Wynn reminisced:

A full moon swung like a yellow pumpkin in the sky, and sheer magic lay over the desert. During the night the newly fallen snow turned to icy casings for the millions of desert bushes spread out in all directions. The sun rose into a clear

sky as I rode up on the hill top, and transformed the desert into a mystic garden of diamond-string shrubbery, glittering and twinkling prisms strung from every smallest branchlet. It came to me very young that perhaps I should never again witness a scene of such delicate, startling beauty.

Hats

Unless this was your place of business, they were rarely doffed, even on visits to the ladies of the camp's "fluzy barns," out back and down the hill. Great care was taken in a hat's selection. Of infinite variety—from Stetsons to sombreros—they made the man. To protect a miner from caving rock, hats were often boiled and reboiled in water thick with starch.

The Barber

The abundance of saloons in western mining camps has been both celebrated and decried—with at times one for every thirty or forty citizens. One explanation was that this was the desert, the domain of thirst. Another was that they served as friendly places of business for mine owners, stock promoters, peddlers passing through, and the like.

Many saloons were "Combinations"—a bar and, variously, a post office, stage stop, cigar stand, bordello, or pharmacy (this last with a "Promise to cure whatever ails you, one way or another"). In this case, it's a bar-tonsorial parlor. His sleeves rolled up, the barber awaits the

next customer for a shave, haircut, or whisker dye. His bottles might dispense imported Brilliantine, or closer to home, the green juice of the pulverized heart of the yucca, an excellent shampoo.

The identity of the men and children in the larger photograph are lost to history—all but the barber. Behind the PABST MILWAUKEE medallion above his head, there is a discernable, *reversed image* of a sign outside the saloon:

_ ILL_ _ E _
_HE B_RB_ _

Kern County voting rolls have it that he would be

BILL LEE
THE BARBER

Of immigrant Irish parentage, Lee was born and grew up in Michigan, then was drawn West, and at the time of the photograph was in his late thirties. In a year or so, he and his wife, Susie, and their two children would forsake the desert for a more comfortable, if less exciting, life operating a Modesto, California, grocery store.

The Game

It is Faro, in the 1890s the most popular game in the West, and for good reason. Its paraphernalia could be home-made and toted under a gambler's arm, and in no more than a few minutes, a fellow new to the game could grasp the basics, ante up hard-won cash, gather his chips, and take the plunge.

On the surface, Faro was a straightforward, innocent-enough game (and may well have been in this photograph). The odds favored the dealer, but only slightly, and there was no apparent way to cheat.

Or so it seemed.

The truth was, there were myriad diabolically inventive ways for the house to shake down players. (For details, see appendix B: Faro and "Bucking the Tiger.")

Here, in fact, was a cautionary tale—an analogy—for life in the Mojave's camps, in Randsburg and those to come. The gold and silver was in the ground; fortunes were to be had, and you appeared to have as good a shot as the next fellow. But you didn't. Mine owners quickly locked up the best land, living expenses were high, and a stunning array of scoundrels—from gamblers to "sure thing" touts—were poised to fleece the gullible.

And yet . . . you could stake your all, and with the chance turn of a rock, as with the turn of a card, strike it rich.

Beat the house. In the morning a pauper, in the afternoon a millionaire. That was the dream, and as the poet Shelley gently asked,

"Tread lightly on my dreams, for they are my dreams."

Randsburg would continued to boom. And, if not wealth, its populace would embrace and enjoy a grand cacophony of entertainments.

The Elite tent-theater hosted traveling shows, and if Shakespeare was in the offing, the audience would accompany the actors in their recitation of soliloquies.

At a rival establishment, "Each night there was a brass band in front to render the opening noise. Bass drum and trumpet, coronet and trombone."

At the edge of the camp, sweet strains wafted from Fiddler's Gulch.

And off in the shadows, unsavory cheers rooted for the coyote or the cock as they fought to the death.

The Fourth of July was the holiday of the year, with, in the year 1899, a celebratory "Parade of Horribles" (with applause and catcalls for a seven-foot, male Goddess of Liberty). A baseball game ensued, then a blindfolded wheelbarrow race. The evening featured a performance by "The Great and Only Sam Beers, the Renowned Fire Wizard."

And now, with the turn of the twentieth century in sight, there was the question: Would the Mojave offer up ever more gold, more silver? Or would hope fizzle and dreams die?

The answer was not long in coming. In 1902, there was word of a new discovery, triggering a wave of wild-eyed excitement. The elusive silver of the legendary Lost Gunsight mine, it would appear, had been located! Not in Randsburg or nearby, but on up in Nevada on the northern border of the Mojave.

Men committed to Randsburg's industrialization—mine owners, mill men, miners with families—would stay on; there was still gold in the ground.

But for the footloose and starry-eyed, a rush was on to the Nevada camp of Tonopah, "greasewood spring" to the local Shoshones. And above Tonopah's scattered campsites, there rose a treasure mountain.

Think of it! The Lost Gunsight! Could it be?

A new century was at hand, and in cooler months the camp's elite sailed hard-packed playas, with their wind-whipped 45 stars and stripes testimony that at least a corner of the Mojave had been settled, exploited, and was reasonably civilized.

THE BIG CASINO

Proprietor Jules Goldsmith (center) was lord of all he surveyed, including (unseen in this photograph) a restaurant, saloon, and betting hall (with direct wires to race tracks in the East). The nine-piece band was first class and the girls were "nice," at least on the dance floor. Prostitutes were available upstairs in little rooms off a horseshoe balcony.

Tonopah

The Big Casino

"Me & Jim Found Tonopah"—with, as proof, sacks of high-grade ore behind the tent.

Small desert animals—from kangaroo rats to badgers—were the prospector's friends; soil ejected from their burrows, when panned, could yield traces of color.

Jim Butler had his burro to thank. The story goes that the animal had wandered off, and, vexed, Jim picked a black rock to throw at it—only to reconsider, for the rock was unusually heavy. Collecting additional samples, Jim took them to assayer Frank Hicks, with the promise of an interest in the discovery if they were worth anything. Hicks scoffed that he wouldn't give a dollar for a thousand tons of the stuff, and chucked the samples onto his dump. Humiliated, Jim retrieved them, and some weeks later, egged on by his wife, Belle, managed to cajole a proper assay. In part, its report read:

SAMPLE 2   SILVER 540 OUNCES.   GOLD $206.70 PER TON.

That would be $1,600 worth of ore per ton.[5] Jim and Belle named the strike the Mizpah, honoring the biblical site where Jacob laid claim to his tribal territory.

5. In 21st century dollars, over $25,000.

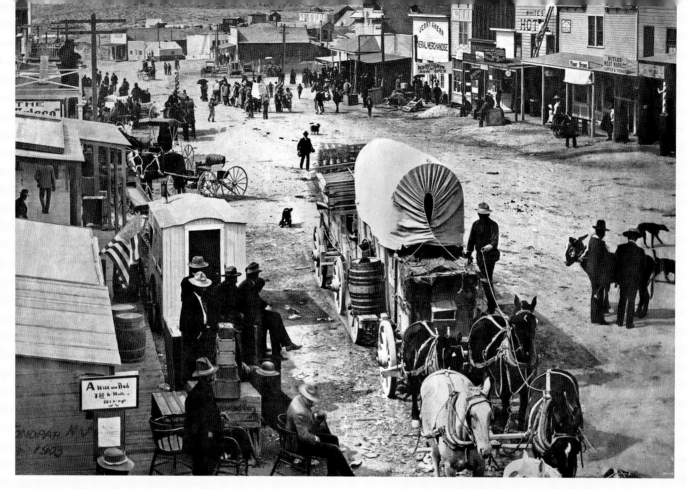

In an image rich in its detail, Tonopah booms. At right, two men discuss a burro. In the lower left-hand corner, a sign advertises "A Nice New Bed/$7.50 a month/50¢ a night." But then, a man would pay dearly for most everything else, with water alone selling for 25¢ a bucket. A saloon in possession of a small washtub charged "First chance $1, second chance $.50, all others $.25."

Look up the street, and you'll spy a troupe milling about.

A few minutes later, waving placards to the beat of a bass drum and snare, the troupe—a traveling minstrel show—parades Main Street, drumming up business.

For what they took to be a very good price, the Butlers sold their claims to Philadelphia capitalists who, with top-drawer mining engineers and massive machinery, would follow an ever-richer Mizpah vein as it plunged 1,700 feet into the earth. Nearby, rival shafts were sunk by the dozen.

It is doubtful that this was the location of the Lost Gunsight. It was far more: a mountain that, in time, would yield in excess of $150,000,000 in silver ore.[6]

Befitting a new century, Tonopah boasted electric power, widespread telephone service, comfortable theaters with local and touring offerings, and the Mizpah, a grand, five-story hotel uptown on Main Street (under construction, upper left in the photograph at right). Life was orderly and reasonably calm. The camp was free of spur-jingling gunslingers. True, Wyatt Earp had drifted in from Tombstone—but to open and tend a saloon.

As a Tonopah matron was to recall,

To dress the part of the frontiersman just wasn't done. Those who attempted it were considered showoffs. [Rather,] it was the high-button coat and bowler hat of the business man, and the leather puttees and campaign hat of the mining engineer. . . . For the most part, Tonopah was a community of city people who lived in rough-board houses and walked unpaved streets, but who dressed and acted as they would in San Francisco.[7]

But look downtown (to the bottom of the photo), and the Old West hangs on in a warren of cribs and bordellos, with their focal point THE BIG CASINO, the "largest hurdy-gurdy house on the West Coast." Celebrated in literature by Jack London, Rex Beach, and Robert Service, THE BIG CASINO was emblematic of Tonopah. It was

Thriving Tonopah, population more than 10,000.

"the Monte Carlo of the Desert," the place where—win or lose—you drank up, taxi danced, and stayed in the mining game.

In contrast to prior workings in the Mojave—Anglo, with a scattering of Mexicans—Tonopah was socially complex. Its citizenry could be sorted by country of origin (with an unusual influx of Czechs and Serbs), by race (with blacks welcome), by religion (with Catholics and Eastern Orthodox prominent), or by lodge (with secretive Masons rivaled by back-slapping Elks—"Masons who drank").

Overall, each had their place on a poor-to-very-rich ladder, with the crowd at the Big Casino occupying the first rung or two.

At the top of the ladder, wives of prominent mine owners, lawyers, and stockbrokers ordered outfits from Paris, and changed them three times a day. They sent their laundry to Reno, a three-week round trip. Chinese servants were desirable, elegant in their service of oysters,

6. Today, as much as two and a half billion dollars.
7. Mrs. Hugh Brown, in her *Lady in Boomtown* (Palo Alto, American West, 1968).

Uptown from the Big Casino, boys "fog about" in a homier locale.

quail, and champagne. Sighed a matron, "The money just rolled over us like a wave that we couldn't stop. . . . We had Dresden china in a tin-cup camp."

An outing took them to the gallows frame of the Mizpah Mine, and down its main shaft to a dancing party.

What a unique event! The music? Three miners playing accordions and a banjo, with muted sounds of pounding hammers and rolling ore cars adding an obbligato from mysterious distances, whence men with candles on their caps appeared and disappeared like giant lightning bugs. . . . Then we had supper: cold chicken, salad, and sandwiches brought in great hampers. . .
—Mrs. Hugh Brown

On another occasion, the elite ladies of Tonopah invited Jules Goldsmith—of BIG CASINO fame—up their hill to offer a violin, cello, and piano musicale. "After listening to Mr. Goldsmith's music, we all declared that we now really belonged 'downtown.'"

On up the social ladder, the Bank Saloon boasts mahogany appointments, flowers, white-jacketed bartenders—and at the rail, swells who visibly swelled.

Up the hill from the Bank Saloon, an oriental-themed Monday salon of the Lunas Clava club. (With "Lunes" for "Monday" and "Clava" for "Club," or so the ladies first thought. They were distressed to learn that, accurately translated, their gathering was a "Monday Cudgel.")

A nocturne for Tonopah.

Far from it. In their airy pretensions, they were oblivious to working stiffs they could thank—but never really did—for their Tonopah fortunes and opulent lifestyles.

Yet, looks can deceive, and life has exceptions. Though she was a Lunes Clava regular, mistake not Mrs. Key Pittman for a social butterfly. As Miss Mimosa Gates, she had, alone and in the depth of winter, driven a dog team the length of the Yukon Trail. She was an accomplished pianist. And she was to take one of the most striking photographs ever in the Mojave.

In August of 1904, Mimosa's husband, Key—she'd met him in the Klondike when their dog teams tangled—had given her a camera, and during a fierce electrical storm the two ventured outside and either mounted it on a tripod or set it on a ledge. Then, reacting to a deafening peal of thunder, Mimosa clutched Key with one hand, and squeezed the camera's bulb with the other, opening its shutter for a number of seconds, even a minute or so.

The result astonished them, for they had had little idea what, if anything, they might have recorded. According to the *Tonopah Miner*, scientists of the day proclaimed the photograph "the most remarkable ever taken."

Tonopah on the night of August 10, 1904. The bolt struck the home of Charlie Reynolds. The lightning seared the wall of the room where he was entertaining two friends, then arced into the kitchen where it melted the better part of a stove before blasting a hole in the floor. Other than being dazed, Charlie and his companions escaped injury.

His wit, as his beard, was Jovian.
Here, he has painted a tie on his shirt.

Tonopah

A Vision of
a Man and His Dog

Is there not something a bit off—distinctly odd—in the image on the facing page? Wouldn't it have been tactful to have the shorter man perched on the rock? Welcome to the droll images of Tonopah photographer Emery Willard Smith.

Smith was born in Massachusetts in 1850, and growing up, he and chum George Eastman were drawn to the new craft of photography. Settling on the trademark "Kodak," George was to manufacture thousands upon thousands of cameras and supply them with film. E.W. was drawn West, first to the Klondike, then in his fifties, to Tonopah. Though he admired George's invention of dry film packaged in rolls, he stuck to—and became a master of—the "wet process," traditional and demanding.

Even if unsigned, Smith's work is identifiable by its whimsy, warmth, and affection. And if there are doubts as to who was behind the lens, look for the dog. Shep, his constant companion, is to be found in Smith's promotional pictures of banks and mercantiles, as well as his group portraits of mine crews, baseball teams, and graduating classes.

Unknown gents at the foot
of a Tonopah mine dump

Though often summoned to photograph the homes of the newly-rich, Smith was fascinated by miner's shacks crafted of flattened five-gallon cans, liquor bottles, and barrels, all in ready supply in Tonopah.

This could have been a routine portrait of a somber-faced crew—but for the magic of a well-received watermelon. Note Shep the dog, lower left.

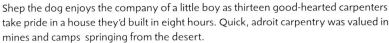

A house gratuitously built in eight hours April 5th, 1908, by 12 members of Carpenters Union No. 1417 U.B. of C. at Tonopah, Nevada, to replace one destroyed by fire, Mar. 28th. E.W. Smith

Shep the dog enjoys the company of a little boy as thirteen good-hearted carpenters take pride in a house they'd built in eight hours. Quick, adroit carpentry was valued in mines and camps springing from the desert.

Shep and a Tonopah tot enjoy a tea party.

For a remarkable forty years in the desert, photography—and the revelation of the human condition—was E.W. Smith's calling.

He was, above all, a portraitist gifted in his ability to, on a glass plate, capture the essence of an individual.

Climbing the rickety stairs to his studio over the Oasis Saloon, his subjects were greeted by a courtly, gentle man with a knack for putting them at ease. Or, if a customer was a curmudgeon or a sourpuss, Smith would make the best of that. So be it.

E.W. possessed but a few painted backdrops, with the stone wall and flower-filled urn of a vaguely classic scene the most popular. Or he'd settle on a stark white or black background (anticipating portraiture later in the twentieth century). The well-worn carpet was ever the same. And he was ever-inventive in his use of simple props—an oriental table and chair, a bowl, a book, a garden gnome, and a teddy bear.

While making the most of the light and shadow cast by a window to the right, the trip of his shutter captured smiles, the sweet flowering of youth, soulful gazes, friendship, hilarity, quiet dignity, glowers, and contentment—from a first year in the desert to near the last.

Unless otherwise noted, the Tonopah images that follow are "subject unknown."

A new friend.

He shot Teddy.

39

41

42

Fashionable "Ardelle," her last name unrecorded.

Good friends.

Shoshone Bill Kawitch,
a shaman, and his wife.

Pity the long-suffering wife.

Frontiersman, rancher, and renegade Jack Longstreet. His long hair masks an ear sheared off in a knife fight. Few dared cross Jack—or, at his feet, his dog.

What a contented, jolly fellow.

A tableaux at Tonopah's Butler Theater. Local girls dressed in doll's clothes honor a visiting prima donna, who had deigned to grace Tonopah with her presence. There's a story that goes with this. The lady's repertoire, it seems, featured provocative songs the likes of "Wouldn't You Like to See a Little More of Me?" and "How About a Little Lovin'?"—which prompted a big-hearted, burly Tonopah fellow to—why not?—accept her invitation. He clambered across seats, and up over the piano to the stage, there to embrace the woman and plant an enthusiastic kiss on her painted mouth. She recoiled and swept off into the wings. Her would-be swain followed. There was a loud smack, and he was propelled back onto the stage, rubbing his cheek. He climbed back down over the piano and sheepishly took his seat.

EMERY WILLARD SMITH, 1850-1941
At the end of his days, near-penniless and unsung.
Chronicler of love, laughter, and hope
on a last frontier.

1904. The Mizpah's hoisting works (the same as opposite). The wheel in the foreground drove a compressor pumping air to miners and their pneumatic drills.

Tonopah

The Ballad of Big Bill

Here, giant pistons hissed and throbbed, Edison dynamos whirred, hoist operators swore, and bells clanged as, via a long copper wire, instructions were relayed from deep in the mine. The first two rings would identify the level sending the message. Instructions would follow:

> 1 bell: hoist ore, run fast.
>
> 3 bells: man or men coming up, run slow.
>
> 7 bells: accident.

A sudden rock fall or an out-of-control "widow maker" drill could snuff out a man's life. But no matter, miners filled the coffers of absentee capitalists, who cared not a whit that underground working conditions were abysmal. Tonopah rock, rich as it was with silver, was laden with silica. And rounds of dynamite reduced silica to a lethal, ragged-edged, glassy dust. Breathe it, and a man's days were numbered.

Still intact, the workings of Tonopah's famed Mizpah mine.

As they sack rich ore, miners' grins belie their fate.

In areas of the Mizpah, silica dust lay on the floor several inches deep. Stir it up, and a man often couldn't see the light of his candle shining on his hand. Miners by the hundreds were incapacitated in a matter of months. Age forty—if you lived that long—was old age.

Silicosis was Tonopah's dark secret. Mine owners made little or no effort to control the dust, and the town's newspapers avoided mention of the disease—even as women and children contracted the malady from silica born home on a husband or father's work clothes.

By its very nature—hollowing the earth—mining was hazardous. Recalled Mizpah foreman Ed Slavin:

> We put timber in there, 18-inch [diameter] timbers every three feet, and they'd be crushed in the morning . . . the whole damn country was moving . . . did you ever see a timber crushed? The rock will break, or the timber will snap and you could hear it moving, grinding, growling . . .[8]

8. Quoted in Robert D. McCracken, *A History of Tonopah, Nevada* (Tonopah, NV: Nye County Press, 1990).

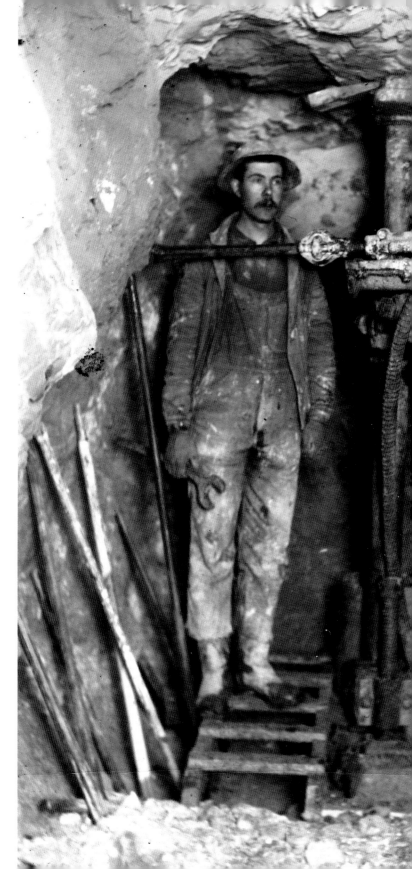

Underground *(left and above)*: Lucky to survive.

Above ground: A table groaning with silver, and in men's eyes, proprietary glints.

A half mile over a ridge from the Mizpah, Tonopah's second richest mine, the Belmont.

In the early morning of February 23, 1911, no one thought to sound seven bells—an accident—in the Belmont Mine. Rather, in the course of what should have been a routine shift change, bullying and incompetence precipitated a disaster that all Tonopah would grieve.

Here is what happened...

4:30 a.m.   Miners at the end of their night shift boarded cages, and on their passage to the surface, believed they smelled smoke. They mentioned this to the hoist operator. He peered down the shaft. Steam (or so he thought) was rising—as was often the case (as in the above photograph). Nothing unusual.

5:30 a.m.   Mike Kuliache, a timber man descending the shaft, swore he smelled smoke.

6:30 a.m.   Bosses for the day shift arrived, and, level by level, sought the source of the smoke. Approaching the mine's 1,166-foot station, they sighted an eerie glow—of flames reflected on the station's rock walls.

7:00 a.m.   In twos and threes, rubbing the sleep from their eyes, eighty to ninety day shift miners straggled up the slope to the Belmont and assembled at the foot of its gallows frame—where they were ordered by Superintendent T.F.M. Fitzgerald to enter the burning mine. If they had a problem with that, they could collect their time and head down the hill.

Fitzgerald then selected several men to join him in smothering or sealing off the fire.

8:00 a.m.   Air throughout the mine was hazy; men took sick. Even so, with the installation of a bulkhead, Superintendent Fitzgerald believed he had the problem licked.

The bulkhead failed. Black smoke billowed through the Belmont. Trapped miners coughed up phlegm. All but blinded, they walked into walls.

8:20 a.m.   A frantic effort—by an inexperienced operator—sought to hoist the day shift clear of the mine.

In the Belmont's hoist house.

Hung over from a night of partying, a critical cage attendant had taken leave of his duties to sleep it off in the "doghouse" adjoining the shaft.

Three long blasts of the Belmont's whistle let Tonopah know that something was terribly wrong over the ridge to the east.

8:30 a.m. But now...."Big Bill" Murphy was on the scene. Burly, twenty-eight years old and known for his Irish charm, he wished one and all a good morning as he strode to cage, and rang for a quick descent. Minutes dragged by. And then the bells: 4-3-3. An order to hoist Big Bill—and the men he'd dragged to the cage!

Down again he went. More miners were saved.

Between gasps to clear his lungs, Big Bill now declared to all assembled, "Well, boys, I've made two trips and I'm nearly all in, but I'll try again."

He swung into the cage and sank from sight. More minutes passed than before, but then the bells sounded, and the waiting crowd cheered. The cage's ascent was erratic. At one point it jammed, requiring the

An anxious crowd gathers at the collar of the Belmont shaft. At the time the photograph was taken, neither double-decked cage was in use.

55

hoist operator to back it off ten feet, and give it a running start to free it of an apparent obstruction. When the cage broke the surface, three barely-conscious men were piled on top of each other. One man's leg had been severed.

And Big Bill had not made it back.

What happened was the stuff of nightmares. Barely able to pull the bell wire, the great-hearted man had collapsed—and his body had been yanked off the cage as it passed a projecting timber, to be mashed between the cage and the shaft.

Big Bill fell hundreds of feet to his death. His body floated two days in the sump of the Belmont shaft. It was so horribly mangled that it would take the coroner three days to make a positive identification.

9:05 a.m. There would be no further attempts to rescue seventeen unaccounted-for miners. Hoist operator Lumley stuck by the rule that a cage could be lowered only when requested by a bell signal. To no avail, topside miners pleaded that smoke-choked men might crawl into the cage and collapse, with no one fit to jerk the bell wire.

Superintendent Fitzgerald privately thanked his stars and God that he—he alone—was the sole survivor of the party he'd recruited to contain the fire.

The cage tender in the doghouse dozed well into the morning.

And Big Bill Murphy became the hero not only of Tonopah, but of the desert West.

WEATHER
Fair tonight
and Sunday

TONOPAH DAILY BONANZA

Today's Silver
Quotation 53

VOL. IX. NO 106   TONOPAH, NEVADA, SATURDAY EVENING, FEBRUARY 25, 1911.   PRICE 10 CENTS.

DEATH TOLL IS NOW 17

Funeral Will Be Held on Monday at 11 O'clock

Holocaust Casts Gloom Over the Entire Camp; Men Sacrificed in Disaster Identified at the Morgue by Friends and Loved Ones.

LIST OF IDENTIFIED

George Dondoro   Clarence David

Expert Arrives in Tonopah Too Late to Prove of Service in Present Disaster-- Reports of Those Believed to Still Be Under Ground are at Variance.

The day of the mass funeral was dismal and bitterly cold; a foot of snow fell. Miners a hundred miles distant had trekked to Tonopah to pay their respects to Big Bill and his fallen companions.

For many—particularly a hard-hit Slavic community—it was
a day of anger. And it was a day of immense sadness.

WEATHER
Snow tonight
and Tuesday

TONOPAH DAILY BONANZA

Today's Silver
Quotation 53

VOL. IX. NO 107   TONOPAH, NEVADA, MONDAY EVENING, FEBRUARY 27, 1911.   PRICE 10 CENTS.

AMID BLINDING SNOW IMMENSE PROCESSION FOLLOWS VICTIMS OF THE BELMONT MINE HORROR TO THEIR LAST PEACEFUL SLUMBER

Unmindful of Wind and Driving Snow Men, Women and Children Filled Every Inch of the
Nevada Theatre, to Hear the Sad Rites for the Departed Miners, Long Before the Ap-
pointed Hour, and Hundreds Who Could Not Enter Sought Shelter Elsewhere to Wait

MEMORIAL SERVICES.

Prelude ... Violin and piano ... Messrs. Goldsmith and Fife
Brass ... ... United Choirs
Scripture ...
Paper and hymn ... ... Rev. P. S. Smithe
Selection—Violin and piano ... Messrs. Goldsmith & Fife
Selection—Violin and piano ... Messrs. Goldsmith & Fife
Funeral Oration ... ... Rev. H. L. Burnham

Brave Men Bowed With Grief Weep as Little Children While Comrades of a Few Days Ago Are Low- ered to Last Long Sleep

**STATE AND PUBLIC BUILDINGS
PLACE FLAGS AT HALF-MAST AND
GOV. ODDIE EXPRESSES SYMPATHY**

The following telegram was received this morning from
Governor Tasker L. Oddie by W. W. Booth of the Bonanza:
W. W. Booth, Editor, Tonopah, Nevada.
I have ordered flags placed at half mast on state and

Big Bill Murphy—"Died While Saving Others"—rests in Tonopah's bleak garden of death.

Splendid, magnificent, Queen of the Camps,
Mistress of countless Aladdin's lamps.
Deity worshipped by kings and tramps,
The lure she is of the West.

Goldfield today, population 250 to 400 (no one is quite sure). The view is from the abandoned right-of-way of the Las Vegas & Tonopah Railroad. This would have been a passenger's first glimpse of the camp sprawling at the foot of Malpai Mesa. A century ago, more than 20,000 hell-bent-for-gold souls thronged this valley. Today, it's a shadow of its former self.

Goldfield

Queen of the Camps

Goldfield stages crowd a rocky draw.

The day was bone-chilling cold. A sandstorm raged. And their outfit was pitiful: "... An old lame black horse, an old black mule, a $10 wagon, a side of bacon, and plenty of mustard and sorry looking baking powder." But down-and-out partners Harry Stimler and Billy Marsh couldn't have cared less as they examined a rock in the vicinity of Rabbit Springs, south of Tonopah, a rock glittering with gold. "Jewelry ore!"

In seven months the pair's Sandstorm claim would bring in seven million dollars, and be proclaimed the "RICHEST GOLD DISCOVERY MADE ANYWHERE IN THE WORLD."

A rush was on—drawing a crowd ever in need of "the next big thing" in the Mojave. The same names would surface in camp after camp. Not only of prospectors and miners, but of tradesmen and women ranging from the Porter Brothers (general merchandise) to Diamond Tooth 'Lil, Fay, and Little Fay (horizontal refreshment).

Fortune seekers, it was reported, could leap from a stagecoach and pan nuggets in the street. Indeed, in the summer of 1904, a correspondent for the *London Financial News* fretted that a pending overproduction of gold could devalue the metal as a standard of international trade.

A "mud wagon" stage arrives in the camp.

The Combination, Goldfield's second saloon (and blacksmith shop). The man with the sagging trousers, second from right, is "Diamondfield Jack" Davis, soon to displace "Doc" Sharp as the camp's resident bad man.

"A town of mud, blood, and corruption." That's how Walter Scott (on the verge of becoming Death Valley Scotty) described raw, early-day Goldfield. The facing photograph (complete with thumbprint) expressed the sentiment. It is, in fact, the setting for the camp's first murder.

As he'd strolled past John Shirley's saloon (1), Curtis "Kid" Kendall rubbed lounging Howard "Doc" Sharp the wrong way. This prompted Sharp to draw his gun, steady it on his hand, and take a shot at the unarmed Kid. He missed. The Kid fled across the street. Sharp fired again, now bringing the Kid to his knees (2). "Don't shoot, I have no gun!" the Kid cried as he staggered on to the cover of a cluster of tents (3), from which "women had run into the street on hearing the firing."[9]

Mortally wounded, the Kid reappeared, to collapse within feet of an ink splotch on the photograph (4).

[**To the reader:** *Before turning the page, note a prominent landmark—Columbia Mountain—to the north of the camp. As a point of reference, it appears in a succession of three remarkable photographs. Sharing the same perspective, they were taken a year apart: in 1904, 1905, and 1906.*]

9. *Tonopah Bonanza*, April 16, 1904. Here is first allusion to Goldfield's soon-to-be-famed Redlight district.

1. Sharp takes a shot at the Kid, misses

2. Sharp fires again, hits Kid

3. Kid seeks cover behind tents

4. Kid collapses, dies

MAIN ST. GOLDFIELD, NEV. JAN. 1904.

Main Street, Goldfield, 1904. Population, at the most, a few hundred.

A year later, Goldfield teemed with life, and was now reasonably law-abiding, with credit due Chief Constable Claude Inman (the title meaning the same as sheriff). When he'd gotten the job, Inman had ridden out of town to round up—and deputize—fourteen of Nevada's rankest "sure shot" backcountry desperados. The deal: become a law-enforcing deputy and past crimes would be overlooked. For good measure, Inman swore in Virgil Earp, late of Tombstone.

To a wave of men new to the camp, the Esmeralda Hotel (left in the opposite photograph) offered beds for six hours—blankets, no sheets—and so, in a day, could accommodate three shifts of miners.

In need of a thirst parlor? Down the street and to the right, twelve bartenders manned the sixty-foot bar of the Northern Saloon. They dispensed over three hundred gallons of whiskey a day, whiskey alone. And it was but a step or a stumble to matching wits with card sharps Billy the Wheel, Crap-a-Jack, or Society Red, under the watchful eye of pit boss Wyatt Earp (in from Tonopah).

Clothing? For prospectors and miners, Shradsky's advertised bargains in Spanish-American War surplus. With the slogan: "Our Pants Are Always Down!"

A cyanotype postcard asks: "Do you recognize me thus?"

Per Larson, photographer of the street scene on the facing page.

Need to keep in touch with loved ones? Further down Main Street, P.E. Larson's Palm Studio offered postcards of local life—of Joshua trees, burros, and mine crews. Or, donning new laced-up boots, khakis, and wide-brim hat, a fellow could pose for a *Carte-de-visite* and post it East. "Dear Auntie, I am fine and dandy". . ."Dear Zora, Have rather changed my vocation. Am doing nicely". . .

But then, up against hard times and with hope on the wane: "Dear Girlie, Everything is going wrong, and I have been in bed again, but am alright now". . ."Well darling, don't feel bad because I am coming home soon, and then look out for a good squeezing."

Main Street, Goldfield, 1905. Population perhaps 8,000. (There's no way to be sure.
The camp's glory days fell between the 1900 and the 1910 census.)

A few miles short of Goldfield, a motor car that had its occupants taking "the ankle express" on to the camp.

5 miles to Goldfield.

The Chrisman *Desert Flyer*, designed and built in Goldfield. Sixty-horsepower and gearless, it took on rough tracks "as she lay."

A third year, and Goldfield sprawled over fifty-two city blocks. Imposing, cut-stone buildings rose from the desert.

A banner slung across the street—MONTEZUMA CLUB HEADQUARTERS—called attention to the exclusive retreat of the camp's newly-minted moguls (upstairs in the building with the tower and flagpole). The Palace Saloon was downstairs, and north across the street, the sign for the Northern Saloon is visible. The "Nixon Block" is on the right a block further—headquarters for Senator George Nixon, who along with his protégé, ex-faro dealer George Winfield, was taking over and consolidating Goldfield's principal mines. As the genial but avaricious senator succinctly put it, "We want it all; we're not here for our health."

When photographed the year before, this Main Street view was chock-a-block with horse and wagons. Now, a motor car is in evidence, with its driver pausing in the middle of the street, perhaps to give ear to the band that's forming just past the "Arcade Music Hall" sign. The auto was one of hundreds to come—Reos, Thomas Flyers, Pope-Toledos, Cadillacs. Indeed, motor stages in short order would replace the horse-drawn variety as they careened across the desert with a "toot, toot, chug, chug, and a terrible horn blast like Gideon's trumpet."

Main Street, Goldfield, 1906. Population: uncertain, possibly as many as 24,000. Now the largest city in the state (but still called a camp).

Main Street, Goldfield. An incandescent lure.

Goldfield gloried in its electrification. With power generated in California's Sierra Nevada—a hundred miles distant—the camp was a beacon for desert travelers. A high-voltage line expedited mining around the clock, and powered the extraction of ore so rich with gold it didn't have to be milled, just loaded in railroad cars and shipped to the Selby Smelter in Oakland, California. At the end of the year, the camp would boast the richest shipment of ore ever recorded, anywhere. It assayed at $12,300 worth of gold to the ton ($308,000 at today's price).

Nevertheless, the wealthier moguls George Nixon and George Wingfield became, the more they were to curse and rail, for the practice of "high-grading" had insinuated itself into their mines. With creative haberdashery, miners would secrete twenty pounds of ore in a double-sewn shirt or socks stretched down trouser legs; five more pounds could be tucked under a false-crowned cap. And there were "big coat men" so laden with ore that, if they stumbled on the walk from their shift to the camp, they required help getting back on their feet.

The stolen ore was accepted in trade for drinks in saloons and as favors for prostitutes. It could be sold to shady assayers—the camp had more than fifty of them—who customarily paid fifty cents on the dollar of the ore's value.

The miners' rationale? "God put gold in the earth for them that finds it." Or, as the Deity Himself had ordained in *Deuteronomy* 25:4, "Muzzle not the ox that treadeth the corn."

High-grading, it was now estimated, siphoned off 40 percent or more of the camp's output.

Never the miner's friend, and now wishing to "break the back of those suckers" and put an end to high-grading, squint-eyed Wingfield was to hire a legion of private detectives from Los Angeles' hard-knuckle Thiel Agency. They kept tabs on miners underground, and undercover after work, plied them with drinks that they might wheedle information as to the identity of crooked assayers.

Still, the gold vanished.

Accessed by seven gallows frames and hoists, the workings of the Goldfield Mohawk Mine. Moguls Nixon and Wingfield saw their 10-cent stock rocket to $20 a share, in what should have been a satisfying 2000% gain. But enough was not enough.

A cocky, contented Mohawk crew. And why shouldn't they be? In a single shift, pilfered ore could make a $4-a-day miner up to $1,800 the richer.

Wingfield and Nixon sought out Goldfield Chief Constable Inman, not to berate him for looking the other way, but to offer him a guaranteed $10,000 a month and on top of that, a 40 percent cut of any stolen ore he might recover. With certifiable bad men at his disposal, Inman was on the case and orchestrated a series of lightning raids.

Inman accordingly boasted of having the "best paying job in the U.S." It netted him over a quarter of a million dollars a year.

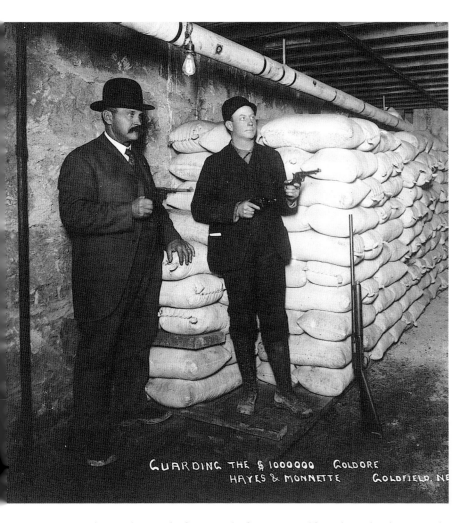

Hired goons kept track of every sack of ore extracted from the Mohawk Mine, and here stand guard in the basement of the John S. Cook Bank.

At the Gold Dog Saloon, the premises of a shady assayer, a spectacular haul of fenced, stolen ore. Note, down the line, the man resting his elbow on the sacks.

ID IN A HIGH GRADE SHOP
IGH GRADE GOLD ORE $1000 A POUND
LARSON
PH
N? 5088   GOLDFIELD
                              NEV

The man with the star: Chief Constable Inman.
He enriched mine moguls. As well, to his credit,
he brought order to a wooly camp.

Unlike nearby Tonopah, Goldfield would boom but a few years. In 1907, the camp was hard hit by Eastern capital's loss of faith in western mining. This triggered a Wall Street panic. In this 1909 image above, note the many buildings, but the absence of traffic. The camp's fortunes were on the decline.

Today, only fading memories remain of the Esmeralda Hotel, the Montezuma Club, the Arcade Music Hall,—all are gone, consumed by a raging 1923 fire that leveled as well the five-story building from which the 1909 panorama was taken. Today, the center building—a rebuilt Elk's Lodge—is the only new construction. Resolutely fireproof, it is the first gunite-coated structure in the United States.

Surviving *(above)*: Mogul George Wingfield's office, the adjoining Cook Bank, and the red brick Goldfield Hotel.

An array of motor stages in front of the Palm Grill, a restaurant promoted as the equal of the Waldorf-Astoria in New York, or for that matter, anything in Paris. Not according to Bonnie Lanagan.

Goldfield

Bonnie Lanagan's Dreadful Night

⊰⊱⊰⊱⊱⊱⊱

Boost, Don't Knock" *was a byword of Goldfield journalism. It fell to Bonnie Lanagan, an out-of-state reporter, to take an unvarnished look at the camp. Her remarkable account, titled "Spoiler Folk of Goldfield,"[10] chronicles a single, boisterous winter's night in 1906. It opens in the camp's smoke-hazed Palm Grill, billed at the time as elite and elegant.*

"Full up," says the muscular waiter, and full up it is. Each small table, with its dusty palm that scatters gray siftings of soil on underdone steaks and amber-filled glasses, its goblet ringed table cloth, is surrounded by men and women, the real makers of this camp that has startled the world. The floor beneath the booted feet looks like beaten dirt. Long time ago, a long time ago in Goldfield, the covering may have been linoleum, but today, under its nightly baptism of wine and its crust of Goldfield mud, it is black and gritty.

10. The title is a nod to a popular novel of the day, Rex Beach's *The Spoilers*, in which gold-seekers wreak havoc on Nome, Alaska's landscape—and each other. Bonnie's article was printed in the Christmas afternoon, 1906 edition of the *Goldfield Chronicle*. Curiously, it was *not* printed in her hometown *Salt Lake City Tribune*. It could well have been deemed too lurid for the Saints.

Sites encountered on Bonnie Lanagan's late night ramble—on a rare, hand-tinted Sanborn Fire Insurance map.

Lower Main Street

Upper Main Street

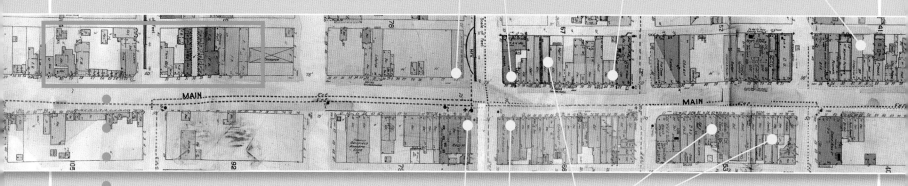

Renowned "four corners" saloons:
Mohawk   Hermitage   Palm Grill   Brown Palace Hotel

MAIN

Palace   Northern   Jewelry stores

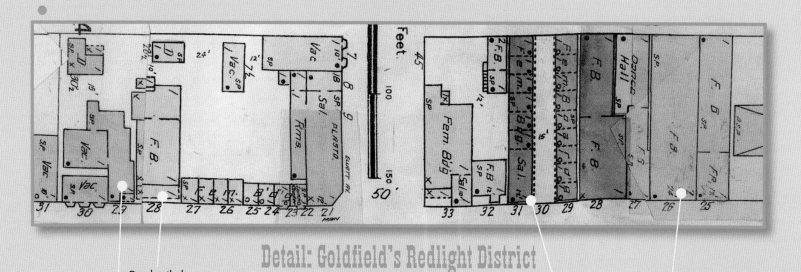

Detail: Goldfield's Redlight District

Den brothel

Ajax's la Parisienne Restaurant

Note "Fem Bldg" and a variety of "F.B."s,
euphemisms for brothels, large and small

Red Top bar
(and double row
of cribs)

Jake's Dance Hall

There are no magnificent characters here. Each table holds its interest, for each man who sits so carelessly and laughs into a woman's eyes so recklessly has dared and suffered for his pile.

Here at the front table gazing ardently at a blonde little creature is a gray-shirted chap whose lined face is puckered painfully in a smile. He's telling her a wonderful tale, the story of his strike. She leans forward, her lithe figure tense in its sheath of black silk princess gown, with diamond earrings glinting like chips of stars . . .

A succession of the Palm's patrons leer and boast and drink too much. Bonnie writes:

Late supper in Goldfield is no dainty affair. Men and women eat, they do not toy with their food. Unlike the babble of city restaurants, sentences fall crisp and terse, and the burden of all the talk is gold. Even the women, the lines creeping in and out of their faces, forget the coquetry and listen. It sounds like stage farce. Huge sums are mentioned so carelessly.

In a stall a man is retelling to a tall, willowy creature in purple how he had made $100,000 that day in his manipulation of the market. And in the next stuffy stall a girl is telling, with a maudlin, teary voice, of the death of her friend. Pneumonia is the death's head at the feast. The spectre has them all scared—hardy prospectors, buxom women, brokers, and stenographers. In this altitude of 6,500 feet pneumonia is quickly fatal for it stops the heart. The slush, the discomforts of the place, where wood is $65 a cord and hard to get at that price, where rooms are never heated, invite the disease, and to quote the large-eyed girl who sits languorously sipping, serious for once: "You order your box when the doctor says you're it."

"Bugs in his air can came and he went to pieces in three hours," the small man in the stall is detailing. "They tried to rush him to Reno, but he cashed in before the train ever got there. Tried to get a cigarette case made for my best girl the other day. Jeweler told me he couldn't get around to it. To busy engraving coffin plates. Nice place, ain't it?"

It was said that "nearly every camp that lasts long enough has its winter of death"—and 1906–1907 was it for Goldfield. Bonnie now takes leave of The Palm, and walks two blocks north to the Brown Palace Hotel.

The dingy lobby fills with a restless, low-speaking crowd. Around the stove the women huddle. It is a Sunday night and a woman who is said to be the wife of a millionaire sits talking to her neighbor, burning her shoes in her effort to get warm. Diamonds blaze in her ears, at her throat, on her fingers; big,

It was a miserable winter. In a photograph taken a month after Bonnie's visit, the Brown Palace is still under construction. Note, as the caption relates, the crowd line up for rations of fuel. Goldfielders had taken to chopping up telephone poles to keep warm.

nut-sized diamonds that twinkle sociably at the diamonds worn by her companion. In the basement downstairs sleep ragged millionaires. The rooms—stalls with partitions of papered thin boards—are furnished with three hooks, a bed, a small tin wash basin and dirty lace curtains. No fire, no comforts, and the proprietor, who looks like a brigand in his wide hat and brown clothes, wants just $4 a night for this room.

Outside the Brown Palace they wade ankle deep in mud. Women pass along the ugly street, with its absurd conglomeration of modern stone office buildings, adobe huts and board shacks, holding their skirts high and disclosing heavily booted feet. Through the seething alkali mud, vehicles churn, throwing up clumps of filth in the faces of passersby.

Bonnie Lanagan heads south on Main Street, passing in short order three shops exclusively given to jewelry: Lord-Cochran, V.L. Kline, and Doane & Rosenthal.

The stores that line the street are all aglitter. Saloons and jewelry shops predominate, the saloons warm and cozy, the jewelry store windows a bewildering blaze of stones.

Goldfielders reveled in diamonds. Perhaps it was that in a bleak, wintry landscape, gold might gleam, but diamonds glittered as a sign that you'd struck it, really made your mark.

Gray shirts and diamonds are the fashion in this camp.

At the intersection of Crook and Main, Bonnie next would have come upon the camp's renowned "four-corner saloons": The Northern, the Palace, the Hermitage, and the Mohawk.

In her narrative, Bonnie makes no mention of these establishments. The best explanation was that, with little exception, they were male preserves. And Bonnie was unwelcome.

What did she miss?

The vehicles drawn up in front of the saloon are cabs; a dozen of them had been imported from the East to lend the camp trappings of civilization. It was the fashion to commandeer one, light a cigar, thrust your feet out the window, and tour the town.

By good fortune, Goldfield photographer Arthur Allen took one, then a second, striking image inside the Mohawk saloon.

The first is to the left.

Next, gaining the confidence—or at least the acceptance—of dealers and players, Allen set his tripod by the saloon's door and held his breath, hoping no one would move, for the shot would be a natural-light time exposure.

With the exception of a poker player studying his hand, suspicious eyes appraise the man with the tripod and camera.

In the Mohawk saloon, a gambling man has his choice of Faro to the left and Craps to the right. Expressions range from wary to near-confrontational. No one smiles. In many respects, Goldfield was a hard-bitten, hard-case town.

AALLEN PHOTO

In a detail of the preceding image, a man on the bandstand holds the sheet music for Navajo, an "Indian two-step" featured in a current Broadway hit. This may have been to counter the notion that Goldfield lacked big-city sophistication.

In Goldfield gathering spots, there was often a circle set aside for expectoration; here the floor is one big cuspidor. To the left, a chair raised on block allow a dealer's assistant to rest his arms flat on the table. Was the game crooked? Likely. (For how to cheat at Faro, see Appendix B.) Up and to the right, there's a blurred cat, evidence of Allen's time exposure.

Catching up with Bonnie . . .

Down the street, away from the legitimate residence district, is the home of revelry and madness, the place where all the good yellow stuff is blown in, answering the lure of the painted ones. Take the first dance hall with every window alight sending out strains of crazy dance music far along the narrow little streets.

Bonnie wasn't shy. Here and back home in Salt Lake City, she was at her best when life edged on the lurid.

Step inside the door. It's getting late now, as respectable Goldfield counts time, but here the merriment is only beginning, for the dance halls do not open until after 11 o'clock. The bar is doing a rousing business. A Gibson-faced man is talking in undertones to a girl in pink—a pretty girl with dark circles beneath her carefully gotten up eyes, circles that tell a tale of too much wine and too little sleep.

The girls wear anything from chiffon to flannelette and only ask for diamonds and brilliant hues. As the hour grows later, the air gets heavier and heavier. Everyone is a little sleepy and a little cross, and when they are not, are either hysterical or quarrelsome.

Here an ungainly prospector makes foolish love.

Bonnie wraps up her account:

The streets are alive. One hears the insistent little click of the roulette wheel, the laughter from the saloons with the thumping of a mandolin or the wheezing of a phonograph stringing along a thin accompaniment to all this madness.

Women are seen all over. Women are not scarce in Goldfield. This illusion, shared by almost every one outside, is a mistake.

The dance hall that Bonnie mentions was almost certainly Jake's. Were his girls available for more than a dance? Almost certainly, considering a handbill advertising "private wine rooms" (accounting for the upstairs windows). Note the adjoining cribs.

For a Good Time
Visit
JAKE'S
Dance Hall
The Pioneer Dance Hall of Goldfield
STRICTLY UNION
PRIVATE ENTRANCE
PRIVATE WINE ROOMS
GOODFRIEND & SYLVIA

Proprietor Jake Goodfriend

A corner bar and double row of cribs in a postcard from the Redlight.

Lower Main Street. In the recollection of Chief Constable Claude Inman, five hundred girls worked the Redlight. A look in the shadows of the three closest cribs reveals their occupants to be Jessie, Sylvia, and Sadie. On down the way: the Den, and Victor Ajax's La Parisianne restaurant, said to serve the finest food in the camp.

A "good for" token for a brothel on down the street.

Only they are most of them of a type, the kind who flock to the rich places of the world, where men have fought and wrested with the earth, men who are willing to throw away the precious yellow stuff for a studied glare from kohl-rimmed eyes.

And the other women? They are just dear little wives tucked away in adobe houses, happy and patient in the midst of privations, for their men are toiling for the gold, that found, means a European trip, the comforts of the East, good clothes and all the luxuries of their golden dreams.

———

As to the Goldfield Bonnie fled, there remains the question: Was the camp that awful, greedy, and grim? The answer is yes—and no, for there was another Goldfield. Of little girls in starched white dresses at the train station. Of families saying grace before dinner. Of schools, hospitals, and a dozen churches.

But what to make of a camp where avarice was counted a virtue? And there was the matter of what Bonnie missed at the far end of Main Street: prominent citizens and their wives "hitting the bamboo" in fourteen opium dens lining Hop Fiend's Gulch.

At the very least, Goldfield was a camp of good times and bad.

Diamonds and mud, fortune and ruin.

Come dawn, Bonnie Lanagan boarded a 6:35 a.m. Tonopah & Goldfield train north to a main line connection to Salt Lake City, where she'd be safely home late the next afternoon.

The downside of "dicing with fortune." The flotsam and jetsam of humanity in a Goldfield gambling hall. The wall is chalked with lineups of horse races at Eastern tracks. Photographer Per Larson has added: "Such is Life in the Far West."

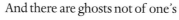
Once home to a miner and his family.

Goldfield

The Ghosts

There are benign, gentle ghosts of the mind, conjured by the sighing of the wind, the swing of an unlatched door, the rattle of tin siding. Ghosts of past glory. Though haunting, they are imaginary.

And there are ghosts not of one's choosing that—some will swear—bewail murder and misery, howl and clatter. They frighten little children, even grown men.

Goldfield lays claim to both.

On a rise north of the camp, a derelict shack overlooks the long-abandoned yards of the Bullfrog Goldfield Railroad. Here lived Johnny Boesch, a dishwasher working establishments like the nearby Santa Fe Saloon, where he survived on table and bar scraps. Yet rumor had it that he had acquired a substantial fortune. The man was worth over a million dollars—or so it was said.

Stories linger in the Santa Fe, the oldest continuously operating saloon in Nevada . . . tales of the miser Johnny Boesch, of one-time bouncer Jack Dempsey, and of blind miner Heinie Miller, who would drink up, then follow a three-mile wire to his workings, where—by taste—he separated gold ore from waste.

Johnny Boesch's cramped and cluttered shack.

The Goldfield Hotel, in its heyday the finest in Nevada. On its opening night, champagne flowed down its front steps and into the street.

Approach Boesch's "miser's shack," peer through a grimy window, and *(opposite)* imagine Johnny home from work, worn and tired—but now riffling through stock certificates and opening royalty checks for mining equipment he had invented, holdings that could afford him a mansion, buy him a fine motor car, even hire a chauffeur. Occasion for parents to whisper to their children, "There goes Mr. Boesch, the envy of all."

And this all came to pass—for the rumors were true!

In his seventies, Johnny Boesch booked passage for a visit to Bavaria, his boyhood home. On the ship he met and courted a well-to-do widow. Marrying on their return to the States, they built a mansion in Los Angeles, and lived out their days in style.

Recalling and imagining the likes of characters such as Johnny Boesch is just that. There's no restless, lurking specter, just a good—and true—story.

As for scarier stuff, there is the camp's grand, forsaken, namesake hotel. Here, if anywhere in Goldfield, is a place that *ought* to be haunted—and sure enough, its shadowy lobby and corridors teem with ghosts (or at least reports of ghosts) that are by turns threatening, mischievous, and heartbreaking.

Off the lobby, the entrance to the "Gold Room," the main dining room. Just inside, a phantom known as "the Stabber" is said to lay in wait and with a large kitchen knife, randomly threaten—but never harm intruders.

The Goldfield's lobby. To the left, one of the first Otis elevators west of the Mississippi. The stairs beyond are the reputed haunt of a pair of prankster spirit children and a midget. Sneaking up on intruders, they tap them on the back, then giggle and dance away. *(Right):* The lobby's reception desk, switchboard, and safe. Catch a whiff of something in the air? Could it be the smoke of George Wingfield's cigar?

Firing the imagination of the suggestible, the Goldfield is rife with creaks, groans, and sighs—the tremolo of mice in a broken-down piano, the panicked flutter of a pigeon's wings. Once inside the hotel, the birds perish, unable to find their way out.

Professsional gambler-become-mining mogul George Wingfield, the hotel's owner from 1908 to 1923.

Could the phantom presence of George Wingfield have something to do with what happened in Room 109?

The story is this:

Wingfield had dallied with Elizabeth, a Goldfield prostitute. Or was her name Gertie? In any case, she was presently with child. George's child, she was sure of it. Fearing a scandal that might impact his business affairs, Wingfield paid the woman to keep her distance.

She didn't.

Elizabeth was soon visibly pregnant—reason for Wingfield to ask her to meet him in the hotel's Room 109. She wanted money, more money. George shook his head, grasped her wrist, and chained her to a radiator. He ordered her given food and water until the child was born.

Elizabeth wept, cried for help. To no avail.

Some say she died in childbirth. Others say that Wingfield murdered her and cast the baby down a basement mineshaft, sunk prior to the construction of the hotel.

In a gauzy white gown, with long hair flowing, a spectral Elizabeth is said to roam the Goldfield's corridors lamenting her lost child—and if you listen carefully, you may hear the infant crying for its mother from the depths of the old mineshaft. Forever beyond her reach.

A fantasy woven of whole cloth?

Not exactly, for there's an underlying reality to the woeful tail.

The woman in question wasn't an Elizabeth or a Gertie, she was a wraith of May Baric, George Wingfield's common-law wife. In 1906, May sought a divorce citing verbal insults, severe beatings, even death threats. Wingfield, she asserted, would pay dearly.

Down the hall to room 109.

George and May's Goldfield bedroom.

Relentlessy, May plagued George, and on one occasion threatened "to pump him full of lead."

George paid no heed. He was invincible, or so he boasted—until in 1908, he was married anew, to a San Jose socialite. In Goldfield, May threatened to sue him on grounds of bigamy. She told a reporter, "He has my diamonds, and Mrs. Wingfield No. 2 is wearing them. It made him crazy when I told him that he would have to settle with me before he could marry anyone else, and he drew a pistol and tried to beat me over the head."

For George Wingfield, known to issue threats backed by one of the several guns he carried, that would have been in character. He would have been sorely tempted to do away with May.

But he didn't.

And at this point, true story and ghost story part company, with colorful invention adding Room 109, the love child, and the mine shaft.

A San Francisco Examiner report of the Wingfield affair—and a rare image of May Baric (top, with George).

Two blocks from the Goldfield Hotel, the bank that safeguarded Wingfield's gold. Reflected in the window: Goldfield's Elks Lodge.

So it is that in present-day Goldfield, no one is all that sure who it is that might have seen or heard spectral Elizabeth. They readily agree, though, that it's all a good story.

Search for the basement mine shaft, and you will search in vain.

And considering all this, one might ask: What need has the camp for scary, trumped-up ghosts when it abounds in truly evocative locales and wistful memories? Of past Goldfielders laughing, crying, drinking, dancing, dying.

They're there. In empty streets, derelict buildings, and windswept cemeteries. There for the imagining.

The Elks Lodge featured a second-floor ballroom, and across a corridor, a meeting room and a well-stocked bar. Here Goldfielders danced until dawn, and raised glasses—"To Elkdom! 'Tis the land where hungry souls can grasp the fraternal hand. 'Tis the land where doubts and fears float off in clouds of smoke from your cigar." And here they would hold services lamenting Brothers who had "departed for God's acre, far across the ferry yonder."

Goldfield's earliest cemetery was unfortunately sited next to the depot of the Las Vegas & Tonopah Railroad—a grim greeting for detraining passengers in the eyes of the camp's boosters. Uniting as "the Goldfield Ghouls," they, by night, exhumed some seventy graves and replanted the occupants a mile from town—a stone's throw from the camp's later, main, cemetery.

The Elks' acre in Goldfield's main cemetery.

The "Graveyard of the Ghouls."

Who was he? What happened?

An evocative headstone in Goldfield's main cemetery. Mildred Joy Fleming had taken sick, and her mother, Annie, was reading her The Count of Monte Cristo. The little girl asked for a glass of water. Annie fetched it, and when she returned, poor Joy was dead. The next day Annie laid her daughter to rest in an unmarked grave; there was no money for a tombstone. A few nights later, torn by anguish, Annie stole a marble block from a school construction site and chiseled it: "Joy." Loading it in her daughter's toy wagon, she trundled it to the cemetery. She then bid Goldfield farewell. Over the years the marker deteriorated, but little Joy was not forgotten. There's a new headstone, handiwork of an Esmeralda County road crew.

Early Rhyolite. Prospects overlooked the camp. "They are so close that we witness a continual bombardment as round after round of giant powder explodes, and echoes and reechoes against the hills that rise majestically on three sides." (The first issue of the *Rhyolite Herald*.)

Rhyolite

"A Hellfire! Strike"

By the turn of 1907, Goldfield's mines were in the hands of syndicates, the largest controlled by George Wingfield. For fortune seekers—ever restless—it was time to move on. And so it was that Dame Fortune beckoned them south to Bullfrog, then Rhyolite, camps on the brink of Death Valley.

Chasing a burro, prospector Shorty Harris spied an unusual blue-green rock—which on closer inspection was flecked with gold. His partner, Ed Cross, was down the slope rustling breakfast, and at first couldn't make out what Shorty was shouting, or why he was so agitated.

Ed cupped his ear, listened up.

"Hellfire! We've struck the richest jackpot this side of the Klondike!"

A camp sprang up: Bullfrog, named for the color of the ore.

Then, a mile higher in the hills, more strikes were made, and a second camp—Rhyolite—was proclaimed, promoted, and platted.

With its citizenry, en masse, hotfooting it on up the hill, year-old Bullfrog was all but abandoned, cause for a May 1906 issue of the *Rhyolite Herald* to crow: "Verily the Bullfrog Croaketh." Rhyolite, on the other hand, would be a camp for the ages, eclipsing all others.

A first saloon. Not long, and there would be forty.

With experience gained in Randsburg, Tonopah, and Goldfield, desert boomers were adept at pulling up stakes and moving on.

A good use for 51,000 empty Rhyolite bottles. The camp's mood was reflected in its whiskey of choice: "Oh Be Joyful!"

Eve, baby Maxine, and Jack Bennett in the summer of 1906. Their bottle home cost them $5.00; they won it in a raffle.

Three competing railroads offered passage to Rhyolite. The camp's population would peak at as many as 5,000 souls.

No ticket required. "Riding the rods" under a freight car.

Fireman Frank Green.

Red Green, night hostler,
Slim Warner, engineer.

For workers on the Bullfrog Goldfield Railroad, some days were better than others.

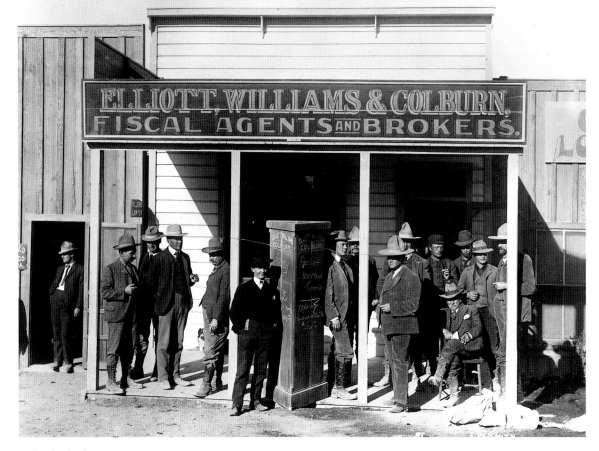

A Rhyolite brokerage.

Preening mining men. They were partial to shiny high top boots, immaculate suits (corduroy in winter, tan twill in summer), and high-crowned hats.

Newcomers would alight in a camp—verily, a city—boasting a modern telephone exchange, two ice cream parlors, three ice plants, a skating rink, four banks, eight hotels, fifteen restaurants, and a thriving, brawling Redlight. In the recollection of prospector and Death Valley entrepreneur Dad Fairbanks:

Every drink shop, gambling or dance hall, had its staff of drag-out men—professional fighters whose business was to bounce anybody that got rough. So, the fellow who started anything usually got his gun taken away from him, got one or two black eyes, and was heaved out of the place. How well I remember a barber we had in Rhyolite. Mike Angelo was his name, and he was an artist at painting black eyes to make them look natural-like. Mike charged three dollars for painting a black eye, or five dollars for two. Some times he painted as many as ten eyes a day.[11]

That aside, there was Rhyolite's truly disreputable element: A blight of self-proclaimed "mining men." They strutted in and out of the camp's twenty-eight stock brokerages.

Not to be confused with actual miners, "mining men" optioned claims, floated stocks, and touted mines (not that a spade of earth had been, or would be, turned). A number cynically "hung paper"—sold shares in prospects they knew to be worthless.

Their clientele, drinking deeply from the cup of self-delusion, believed Rhyolite was destined for a glorious future, that it would outshine Randsburg, Tonopah, Goldfield, anything before.

No matter that not one of the camp's many mines was operating in the black.

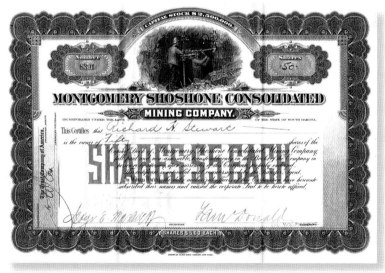

11. Ralph J. "Dad" Fairbanks, "My 73 Years on Southwestern Deserts," *Touring Topics* (Automobile Club of Southern California), vol. 22, no. 6 (June, 1930), p 23.

May, 1907. The Sells-Floto circus parades the length of Golden Street.

The circus parade passes the Porter Brothers' general store. Rhyolite would witness feats of Sampson, "the strongest man in the world" and Mlle. Hilda, "the elastic Venus." They'd marvel as horses walked tightropes and Zietz's "Giant Performing Elephants" rode bicycles. *(Below)*: What remains.

It was a gala day when the Las Vegas & Tonopah Railroad brought the circus to town—and the populace cheered the elephants.

"Seeing the elephant." It was an expression dating to the 1849 Gold Rush to the foothills of California's Sierras. It meant seeing for one-self what the fuss—the headlong excitement—was all about. Then, like as not, returning home no richer and a lot poorer. And given to shaking one's head and muttering:

"I've seen the elephant."

So it was with Rhyolite. The same month the circus performed and folded its tent, Rhyolite mining stocks faltered, then slid and tumbled on the San Francisco Exchange. Enough of puffery, where were the dividends? What of reports that the deeper the ore, the less the assay?

What of growing suspicions that fast-talking "sure thing" mining men were more interested in seeking gold in the pockets of the gullible than in digging it out of the hills?

Mines closed. Merchants, gamblers, light ladies, and honest miners—as well as mining men—moved on.

By the end of 1907, the wonder camp had all but gone bust.

Earl Clemens, editor of the *Rhyolite Herald*, was to have a last word. Proofing a typical "Boost, Don't Knock" front page, he reached for a blue crayon. The edition would be the last. He scrawled . . .

THE RHYOLITE HERALD

With which is combined THE BULLFROG MINER

VOL VIII. NO. 8   RHYOLITE, NYE COUNTY, NEVADA, SATURDAY, JUNE 22, 1912   TEN CENTS A COPY

Their smiles belie a shaky enterprise, considering that it was the town, not its citizens, that the Grim Reaper had in mind. In the boom year of 1907, thirty-two Rhyoliters expired, on average one every ten days. Not encouraging, if you're a mortician. The next year, as the population plummeted, the count was ten souls for the entire year. It was time to pack up and join the exodus.

In 1909, the Rhyolite branch of Goldfield's John S. Cook Bank.

In the 1930s *(above)* and *(below)* a hundred years after the bank closed its doors.

Rhyolite, 1908. A metropolis, even as the camp was emptying out.

RHYOLITE, NEV.

Rhyolite today.

FROM LADD MT. FEB. 1908

Greenwater

Greed and Fraud

To the east of Death Valley, the Funeral Range capped with snow.

High in the Funerals, windblown, blanketed with snow, the little camp shivered. Firewood was scarce; dinner was out of a can and cold. There was drink, though, a sufficiency of that. And dreams.

In a month or two at the most, Greenwater's denizens were convinced, the misery would be worth it, for the camp's promoters assured them that they were located square in the center of huge ledges of high-grade copper cropping the surface over a six-hundred square mile area. If so, as a contemporary *Copper Handbook* noted (with a touch of skepticism) ". . . this wonderful property would carry 200,000,000 tons of refined copper . . . more copper than all the developed copper mines of the world!"

For the snowbound men in drafty tents, who needed Rhyolite—or gold even? Copper was the ticket.

Yet, for all its promise, little came of the Greenwater. The camp folded the next summer. All that remains are a dozen slapdash stone foundations amidst acres of broken bottles. And, to keep the stench of rotting food clear of the camp, there's a tin can dump up a sandy draw.

(X) Cloudman Residence.
(2.3.4.5.6.8.10.) Saloons.
(7.9.10.11.12.) Stores.
(13) Water Tank & Water Wagon.
(14 & 15) Lodging houses.
(16.17.& 18) Restaurants.
(19 & 20) Barber Shops.
(21) Shoemaker's Office.
(22) Had Thanksgiving Dinner 1906.
(23) Post Office
(24) "Greenwater Times" Office.
(25) Miners Hall
(26) Townsite Office & Proposed Bank.
(27) 200 yds to Schwab mine.
(28) Other mines.
(29) 1.5 miles to Clarks mine & Townsite
(30) 2 miles to Ramsey & new Greenwater Town
(31) My present field of work.
(32) Automobile.
(33) Nash & Wallace Co. Office.
(1 & 2 & 13 & 9) Only business houses here
      when I arrived.
(34 & 35 & 36) barns.
(37) Hay & grain store House (Notice its empty)
Picture taken after 1st snow storm.
          Dec 1906.

In late 1906, the camp of Kunze was renamed Greenwater—for the alleged coloration of the nearest spring. A showing of copper? *(Left):* A guide to Greenwater inked on the back of the above photograph.

Filled with sand, a scattering of five-gallon cans once anchored a Greenwater tent.

What exactly happened?

The answer, in a word: fraud. A monumental fraud, the handiwork of a host of desert-savvy mining men.

And greed. As dawn banishes darkness, greed wonderfully dispelled any questioning of Greenwater's extravagant claims. Investors who should have known better were duped, including vaunted moneyman Charles Schwab, President of U.S. Steel.

In good measure, the swindle was abetted and perpetrated by a lively, pocket-size monthly that was hand-printed in a Greenwater tent. At first glance, *The Death Valley Chuck-Walla*, appeared a folksy, straight-talking "Magazine for Men"—men drawn to Greenwater. In the spring of 1907, they came in droves, upping the populace from seventy to a thousand.

On second look, the magazine was a cleverly crafted appeal to Eastern investors. At the behest of the camp's mining men, the *Chuck-Walla* was distributed to stockbrokers across the country. The result: $6,000,000 committed to forty-eight companies poised to exploit Greenwater's "iridescent dream."

When it became apparent that there was an absence of huge ledges cropping the surface (as initially promised), the *Chuck-Walla* was certain *they were underground,* awaiting only the miner's pick. Over a three-month period, the magazine strung along anxious investors with:

In the tailings of the Schwab Merger mine, a copper-stained but worthless rock. Very little copper could green up acres of apparent ore. A miner's saying went, "Swallow a penny; take a leak; stain up a County."

Work is going along merrily . . .

There are showings to warrant the expenditure . . .

The value of the mines is greater this month than it has ever been before . . .

There is nothing like it . . .

But then, overnight, the hype was up in smoke. Mining expert Oscar Adams Turner set foot in Greenwater, and two hours later was at the telegraph office. The message—to Eastern brokers, to the financial world: Do Not Use My Name Any Further Stop There Is Nothing Here Stop Turner.

Everyone, from armchair investors to mighty Charles Schwab, had been duped.

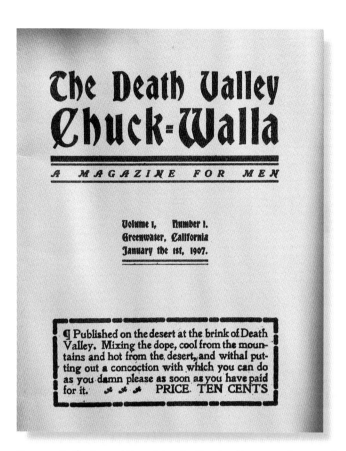

The Death Valley Chuck-Walla

A MAGAZINE FOR MEN

Volume 1,   Number 1.
Greenwater, California
January the 1st, 1907.

¶ Published on the desert at the brink of Death Valley. Mixing the dope, cool from the mountains and hot from the desert, and withal putting out a concoction with which you can do as you damn please as soon as you have paid for it. ❧ ❧ ❧   PRICE. TEN CENTS

Common to the Funeral Mountains: the lizard and its namesake magazine.

Reeling from a one-two punch—the chimera of Rhyolite, the swindle of Greenwater—not only mining stocks, but all stocks tumbled on exchanges from San Francisco to Wall Street. Banks failed. Plungers shot themselves. It was the "Panic of '07."

For years, the Chuck-Walla's press was abandoned in the sand. It's now at Death Valley's Furnace Creek Ranch.

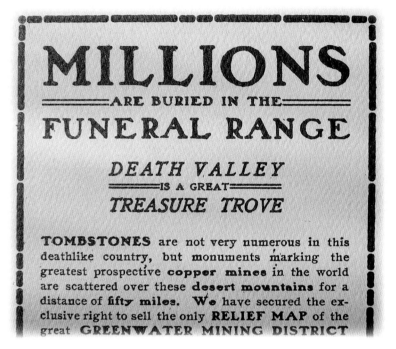

MILLIONS
ARE BURIED IN THE
FUNERAL RANGE

DEATH VALLEY
IS A GREAT
TREASURE TROVE

TOMBSTONES are not very numerous in this deathlike country, but monuments marking the greatest prospective **copper mines** in the world are scattered over these **desert mountains** for a distance of **fifty miles.** We have secured the exclusive right to sell the only **RELIEF MAP** of the great **GREENWATER MINING DISTRICT**

With a total output of $2,625 in copper ore—a single carload— Greenwater was declared "the swindle of the century." And the swindlers? A specialist in bogus copper issues, broker Joseph R. Weil (known for his canary attire as "The Yellow Kid") was to assert:

"I don't consider anything we did as phony. It was imaginary."

Greenwater miners. They had blasted and shoveled, all for naught. Yet there was promise anew in the great shimmering gulf westward over the Funerals from Greenwater. In the year the bogus camp rose and fell, the *Goldfield Tribune* proclaimed: "Death Valley Full of Gold."

GREENWATER TIMES AND
POST OFFICE,
GREENWATER CAL-1906

Recruited to publicize Greenwater, Goldfield-based photographer Per Larson had a cross-section of the camp's citizens pose with the tools of their trade. Miners, left to right, sport a shovel and a pick, and a prospector has his burro. Behind, staffers of the *Greenwater Times* study their output. A surveyor leans on his transit. A carpenter holds his saw.

GENERAL VIEW
OF
GREENWATER, CALIFORNIA.

1 C.M.SCHWAB'S
2 GREENWATER & DEATH VALLEY MINING CO.
4 EL CAPITAN MINES.
5 BLACK JACK MINES.
6 CALUMET
7 GOLD NOTE MINE.
8 BETHUNE MINE.
9 LUCKY BILL MINE.
10 GOVERNORS MINE.
11 BLACK ROCK MINE
12 IRON CROWN

13 GLADSTONE MINE.
14 MAGNA CHARTA MINE.
15 WEST SIDE MINE.
16 HUB MINE
17 FORTUNE MINE.
18 COPPER BOTTOM MINE.
19 COPPER PLATES MINE.
20 PATSY CLARK MINE, GREENWATER FURNACE
21 CREEK MINING CO.

GENERAL VIEW OF
GREENWATER CALIFORNIA
SHOWING THE WORLDS GREATEST COPPER BELT MOUNT

N° 4204.
R.E. LARSON PHOTOS GOLDFIELD.
ESMERALDA COUNTY.
NEVADA U.S.A

Per Larson's panorama of Greenwater. Note the explosion set off between the camp and #10, evidence of something happening.

Greenwater (or Kunze) a hundred years later. With the exception of the Schwab Merger mine to the left
(#1 above) there's a remarkable absence of tailing where Per Larson had identified workings.

Death Valley

Vale of Illusion

A Death Valley icon: "A single blanket jackass prospector."

Wrote Ed Busch, a prospector out of Rhyolite:

We reached the summit of the Funeral Mountains at sunrise. Death Valley, somber, silent and forbidding as a sepulchre, lay like a serpent thousands of feet below. I viewed the desolate scene in awe. In the very atmosphere there was a warning. "Thus far and no further," it seemed to say. "Enter not into this Valley of earth where prayers are not answered and pity is a stranger."

Its restless sands deceive with appearance of stability, but when you trust yourself upon them they shift with the winds like waves of the sea. Your feet give way under you, your tongue swells with thirst, and your cries for water are lost. If you persist in your course, you shall pay the penalty for your rashness. Your suffering shall overcome you. The chord upon which hangs your reason shall snap, and you shall wander among these sandy wastes a raving maniac until

A wind-swept, sun-scorched landscape in which men, if present, were of little consequence.

A daily challenge: prospectors secure their kit with a double-diamond hitch.

death shall have stopped your feet, and your body shall lie in the sands a warning to others![14]

Nevertheless, there was a draw to the place. The valley beckoned and seduced a man. For did it not stand to reason that if great riches were to be found in the region, they would not be in the mountains overlooking Death Valley, but on down in its blazing, hidden, hellish heart?

The answer was that, *no*, this didn't stand to reason. But, be that as it may, in 1908 there was no dissuading some 4,000 to 6,000 treasure seekers. The truth was that, in the region—or even the entire American West—there was no place else to look. Death Valley was a prospector's last great hope.

Descending the Funerals, they followed "shirt tail" routes marked by strips of colorful cloth affixed to cactus and mesquite. Down and down they'd go, to the rhythm of crunching hooves and feet, and slaps to dispel insects alighting on noses and buzzing in ears. Loose rocks echoed down the slope.

Up and up the temperature would relentlessly climb—as much as 50 degrees Fahrenheit from dawn to midday. In the summer, prospectors swore they could hear the heat sizzling—at up to 180 degrees underfoot (the equivalent of 124 in the shade).

Long suffering animals bore the essentials of their calling: Hammer, pick and shovel, gold pan, piston mortar, battered cooking pots, and a blanket, not for warmth but to lessen, "very materially, the chance of getting rattlers for bedfellows" (according to a *Prospector's Manual*). For sustenance, there would be flour, beans, rice, bacon, potatoes, onions—"onions eaten raw are a great promoter of good health on a prospecting tour."

14. Sadly, Busch failed to heed his own advice. He perished on a day when, in the shade, a thermometer hit its limit of 136 degrees and shattered, in a week of the hottest weather ever recorded, anywhere on the earth.

"Hades with the lid off." From the crest of the Funeral Range, a party gazes down into Death Valley. They turned back.

It is an outcropping, but is it worth anything?

They took up the search . . .

A prospector would scramble up to an promising outcrop, and discover it already staked.

He'd chase down a runaway burro.

He'd wolf down the same thing he ate yesterday and the day before.

He'd trudge on.

He'd hammer a yellow stringer, hoping it was malleable. It cracked. Fool's gold.

The man's eyes would burn. He'd be cotton mouthed. He'd feel the heat stiffening his joints. His feet would roast.

It got a fellow down.

A month or so of cracked lips, foul water, dismal food, and unyielding geology—and that, most often, was it. Only the hardiest—only the delusional, some would say—remained, over flickering campfires, to debate lost mines and phantom lodes. The Lost Breyfogle and the Lost Gunsight were out there.

Somewhere.

"The Death Valley Terrapin," Shorty Harris was the region's most famed—and most loquacious—prospector. To anyone who'd care to listen (and many who'd not), he would recount his Bullfrog-Rhyolite discovery, and better yet, the one he'd just made, the one he'd reluctantly but willingly sell. And in his come-on there lay a secret. Certainly, he would have made a strike. He'd take a buyer right there, and offer him a sample to take to an assayer. He'd wonder out loud that if this was what broke the surface, imagine what was hidden below! As the saying went, "the deeper, the richer." And this indeed may have been the case in Tonopah or Goldfield, but not in Death Valley. There, more often than not, a surface showing petered out a few feet down. Well aware of this, Shorty would own up later in life, "I have found pockets that held as much as $1,000 in gold, rich with ore with 'the eagle stamped right on it.' I typically panned out a fair-sized stake, and then sold the mine while the showing was still good."

The little man—4 feet 10 inches—in the stovepipe hat is Shorty Harris.

Dense and whitish-blue, the air would dance and glow and bake. The wind would rise, and sandstorms would rage for days on end. "It was like a blizzard of Dakota, with the grit of broken volcanic rock in the place of snow. No man could face it."

Shorty Harris and Death Valley Scotty.

As Death Valley Scotty (Shorty's rival for desert limelight) was to sum it up, "There's many a good mine that's been spoiled by a pick."

Death Valley Scotty (Walter Scott) was in on Shorty's secret, and he had one of his own: a fabulously rich mine. It was, Scotty hinted, secreted up a canyon in the Funerals—or was it the Panamints? He was the envy of all and kept them guessing, with his message to the curious: "Don't let me catch you following my trail into the mountains. I'm warning you. I'll take my own back trail, and you'll never live to tell the story."

A lot went into being Scotty. Consider the figure he cut. His Texas-peaked hat was his trademark, as was a red tie. A 30-40 Winchester was slung from his saddle. Out of sight, he packed a sawed-off shotgun fitted with a pistol grip, and a "throw away" pistol tucked in his shirt. If he was to be believed, a saddle bag held a jar of nitroglycerin crystals to blow up a trail behind him. "Touch it off. It would blow the whole mountain down."

Scotty's boots had four buckles. They described, he was to confide, his courtship and disdain of moneyed Easterners. "Parlor Plungers," he called them:

FIRST:	Ketch 'em.
SECOND:	Skin 'em.
THIRD:	Soak 'em all.
FOURTH:	Keep out of jail.

At the end of the desert day, Scotty was hardly a prospector, but rather a folksy scammer, a clever swindler.

There was no secret mine.

But there had to be! Wasn't Scotty seen carting thousands of dollars worth of gold amalgam—in sacks bound with dog chains—to banks in Goldfield, Dagget, and San Bernadino?

Only if you believed him.

Flapjacks and coffee on the floor of Death Valley.

And that roll of hundred dollar bills he was forever flashing? It was "upholstered" with ones.

Scotty was Death Valley's consummate illusion. A con artist. And mean. If anyone in the crowd that cheered him when he ventured to Goldfield had tried to filch his roll of bills, he would have found the pockets of his Ulster overcoat lined with fishhooks. In the early morning, as the camp's newsboys delivered papers, Scotty would scatter nickels and dimes on the ground, and as the little kids dove for them, delight in stamping on their fingers.

Yet the secret mine myth lived on (still does), even as, brought to trial in Los Angeles, Scotty weepily admitted, "Between chasing my jackass and rustling grub and water, I didn't have much time for prospecting. I didn't keep books, didn't find any gold, so what the hell is the fuss about anyway? I ain't got nuthin', and I never had nuthin'."

Death Valley Scotty excepted, there was a band of prospectors who dreamed—and wandered—ever on. Their number included Clarence Eddy, a self-proclaimed "poet-prospector." On the trail he would jot in his pocket notebook . . .

Crossing Death Valley, prospector Chester Pray. He and Clarence Eddy were off-again, on-again partners.

Some win by luck, some win by pluck
And some win not at all . . .

While life endures, the spirit lures
And gold allures us all . . .

And golden themes and golden schemes
And golden dreams abound.

A dust-caked, tattered-jacket fraternity, Death Valley's prospectors had both a wandering poet—and a genteel godfather, the Frenchman Old John LeMoigne. Old John had found his way to the Valley back in 1884, and came to love life in the desert as no one before, and few since.

MARBLE CANYON.
IN DEATH VALLEY

COPYRIGHTED 1907.
T. J. BACK.
RHYOLITE, NEVADA

Eddy in a portrait taken in Rhyolite.

In the Cottonwood Mountains (north in the Panamint Range), Chester Pray (along with Clarence Eddy) on his way to visit John LeMoigne.

Old John's camp. He was a good cook. He tended a vegetable garden, kept chickens—and welcomed fellow prospectors to while away a few days swapping stories or reading a book from a shelf stocked with classics. He dusted them daily.

Not far from his camp, Old John reduces promising rock to dust, and pans it for color. To a visitor, he was "calm, polite, philosophical; with polished manners, a ruddy smile, all the ways of a gentleman, He was a dreamy sort of fellow, quite content to live alone and let the world go by."

If they hadn't made a fortune, they were willing. Their identities, their good or bad luck, and what came of them are lost to history. Was one Chuckwalla Mike? Another the Duke of Wildrose Canyon? Or the asthmatic Whispering Kelly? Or Radiator Bill, on the prowl for uranium?

Crossing paths, prospectors George Bart and John Cook
share a rare moment of cheer.

Ever hopeful.

Had they taken leave of their senses? In the opinion of the county seat's *Inyo Independent*, Death Valley was "the world's largest underground insane asylum . . . the Ultimate Thule of the neurotic."

In the preceding gallery, a prospector's gaze ranges from hapless to mildly hopeful. They're a solemn lot with a dreamy, dazed gaze, as if looking through the photographer to a distant hazy ridge—or the next, where surely their fortune would lie. No one smiles. Why should they? If they'd struck it, they'd be off celebrating in Goldfield or even San Francisco.

Even so, when the money ran out, they'd return to the valley and, as poet-prospector Clarence Eddy saw it, a life of "blanching hell, solitude, thirst, heat, rattlesnakes, and general dangers."

Very real dangers.

There were snakes of course, and sunstroke or "thermic fever." Its onset was insidious in that it impacted a man's mind well before his body, with the consequence that he'd become careless, even reckless. The stages of sunstroke are documented in Death Valley lore. A sampling:

A roaring in the head is said to presage the insanity that makes them run wild . . .

Of these thirst-driven-mad men, after they get to a certain stage, the first thing they do is to strip stark naked and commence to run. Afterwards they drop down on the sand and vigorously paw into it, like a dog.

When reason departs out there, death soon follows . . .
When found he begged to be shot.

"You find fellers dead down there," an old timer was to muse, "And they don't die of thirst, either. Sometimes there's water in the canteens. They just go crazy. She [the valley] gets 'em."

And, there was no doubt about it, intense loneliness went with the territory. A man would dwell on the fact that he might be the only soul in a hundred square miles. If anything went wrong, who would minister to him—or mourn and bury him?

As Clarence Eddy the poet-prospector lamented,

There are many lives so lonely,
Lonely through all the lands.

Loneliness, heart-aching and desperate. It was the price of a search for riches in which . . .

In place of a substance a shadow
is better than nothing at all.

A crossroad in the southern end of Death Valley, west of Saratoga Springs.

"At first they [the physical surroundings] are formidably and strangely repellant, then they are endurable, and then they come to hold you with a weird fascination. The glaring, burning hues of the earth and sky, the utter desolation of the barren mountains seem to be softened and blended in a more pleasing mood the more you see of them, and yet there is always that awed feeling of a soul lost on the waste." *(Fred Wamsley, a British visitor.)*

Prospectors gather at Saratoga Springs.

Photo by A. R. Pearl

Death Valley

Flyspeck Camps

For souls that made Death Valley prospecting their life's work, there was a growing reluctance to journey to "the outside" even if they'd made a strike and a sale, and an extended toot was in order. They preferred "the inside" and a circuit of settlement—with populations of a half dozen to two or three hundred—that between 1908 and 1915 ringed the valley.

To the south, Saratoga Springs offered a welcome respite. In the summer months, a fellow could dip a tattered sheet in the oasis' dark waters and wrap himself clammy and mummy-like in the sand, so that evaporation's cool might bring him fleeting leave of his chosen hell on earth. At midnight the temperature could be in excess of 120 degrees.

Midway up the valley, at Furnace Creek Ranch, an eight-foot diameter, water-powered fan cooled wayfarers. Here, as elsewhere on the valley floor, housekeeping was a challenge. Wood warped and splintered. Water barrels, if drained, snapped their hoops in an hour. If uneaten, meat hopelessly spoiled in the same amount of time. Flour bred worms. And sand sought every crevice.

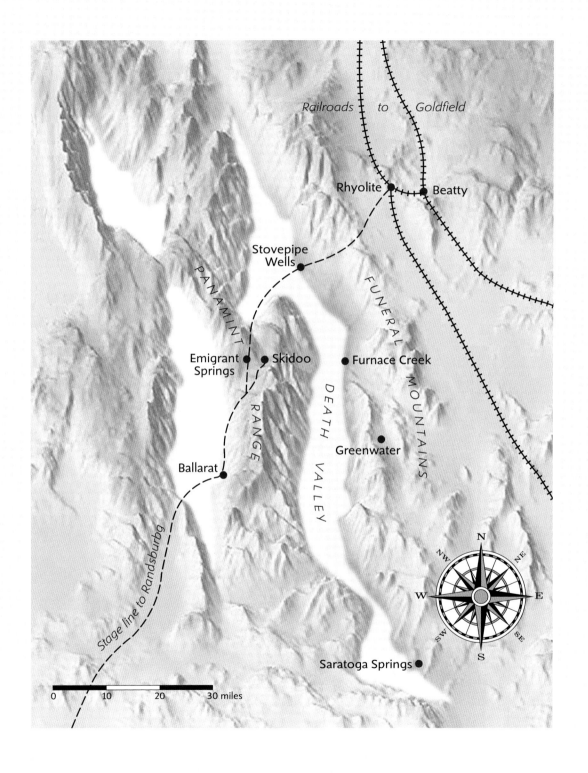

Death Valley's
Way Stations
and Camps

Railroads   to   Goldfield

Rhyolite • Beatty

Stovepipe
Wells

PANAMINT

FUNERAL

Emigrant
Springs • • Skidoo

Furnace Creek

RANGE

DEATH

MOUNTAINS

Greenwater

Ballarat •

VALLEY

Stage line to Randsburbg

Saratoga Springs •

N
NW   NE
W   E
SW   SE
S

0   10   20   30 miles

Further north, a stovepipe stuck in the sand—marking and protecting a critical spring—was a beacon to the parched prospector.

When a road was graded from Rhyolite across Death Valley to the promising new strike of Skidoo, isolated Stovepipe Wells came into its own. Wagons of the ever hopeful rattled though, and soon a stagecoach line. A saloon, big canvas tent store, and a bathhouse opened for business. It was a stretch to call the settlement a camp; it was more a way-station. A true camp, it was held, would have a Wells Fargo office and a bordello. Nevertheless, Stovepipe Wells boasted Death Valley's very first telephone.

Stagecoaches making the run up from Stovepipe Wells up into the Panamint Mountains to Skidoo changed horses at Emigrant Springs where passengers could dine at Buster Brown's chop house. Or at Jack Hartigan's thirst parlor, they could down drinks in the company of prospectors who had come to file claims with a resident County Recorder.

A rare 1908 image of Stovepipe Wells (five miles northeast of today's settlement). But for his shadow, the photographer is unknown.

Aftermath of a winter storm at Emigrant Springs, across the valley from Stovepipe Wells. Chester Pray was one of the very few who would strike it rich in the region.

141

A newspaper at the time reported that Skidoo "grew in a flat little hollow but it did not nestle because a mining camp does not nestle. Like a tin can, it lies where it is thrown."

Then it was on to Skidoo, where it was deemed "only a matter of time" before the Santa Fe laid tracks to this, "the richest gold strike in the desert, and that means the richest on earth."[13]

The boast aside, Skidoo was a quiet, even sleepy settlement. Every so often, the hand press of the *Skidoo News*—shamelessly proclaiming the camp's glory—would clatter away in a tent. A dog or two might bark, but then doze undisturbed in the midday sun. On rare occasion, the raucous cries of the Skidoo Babe or Jane Doe Blondy (her name when booked for naughty behavior) arose from one or another of four saloons.

The album on the next page cites Scrubby the mule as an "Unofficial tamer of loud bad bullies," and in Skidoo a bully there was—Joe "Hootch" Simpson. In his past a ne'er-do-well bum, pimp, and petty thief, he'd recently acquired a modicum of respectability as part owner (and prime customer) of Skidoo's Gold Seal saloon. His fondness for drink is evident in a card he had printed up for his friends *(opposite)*.

On April 20, 1908, Joe "Hootch" Simpson would expand his resume, adding "cold-blooded murderer." Bamboozlement and fraud aside, Death Valley's camps had been surprisingly crime free. Until now.

On that dusty morning, the curtain was to part on Skidoo as a stage, and the enactment of a melodrama out of a dime novel—excepting that what follows actually happened, with action and dialogue reported by five, first-hand participants.

13. The *Rhyolite Herald,* March 1, 1907.

Hootch Fighters' League No. 4
HEADQUARTERS AT

The **G**old Seal Saloon

WINES
LIQUORS
CIGARS

OAKES & SIMPSON, Prop'rs.
SKIDOO, CALIF.

The bearer, Mr. *Lester Polhamy* having displayed all the necessary Hootch Fighting qualifications, is entitled to a free drink at any old time or place in any hootch dump on earth. (Provided, etc.)   Signed:

_____ President   *Fred Oakes* Treasurer
NONE BUT WHITE LABOR EMPLOYED   (OVER)

Rules Governing Hootch Fighters' League No. 4.

Rule 1—Any brother refusing a drink shall be expelled from the League.

Rule 2—Two members constitute a quorum.

Rule 3—The main object of the League is to procure hootch, whether you beg, borrow or steal it. Get it!

Rule 4—All initiations shall take place at **The Gold Seal Saloon**, corner of First and Skidoo Sts. Skidoo, in front of the bar being the proper place.

Rule 5—No brother shall retire for the night while there is a drink in sight.

Rule 6—The password of the League shall be "You Bet I Will."

Rule 7—All hootch dumps shall look alike to members of the League.

Rule 8—Any brother finding another in distress shall procure, in any way, a sufficient number of drinks to alleviate the suffering of the unfortunate brother.

95.12.43

A period scrapbook offers facets of nothing much going on: a lounging man, his left eye possibly damaged in a mine accident; a good-sized but not terribly productive mill; the operation's cyanider; and the mule "Scrubby."

Prologue

Mid-morning.

The Skidoo Trading Company's mercantile operation and R.E. Dobbs' bank shared quarters. Stepping up to the bank's counter, Joe Simpson asked for twenty dollars.

DOBBS: "Joe, you know how your account stands."
SIMPSON: "I don't care. I want it anyway."

His demand garnering a stony stare, Joe shouted and swore, prompting the owner of the adjoining store, Jim Arnold, to intervene and prevail upon him to leave. A muttering Joe stalked out, to roam Skidoo looking for trouble.

What Joe could use, Jim Arnold decided, was a cool-out in Skidoo's jail. He sent for the camp's constable, at the time tending to business several miles distant.

Prior to Joe Simpson's fatal tear, Jim Arnold, left, takes his ease at what ominously looks to be a fenced grave.

Act I

Early afternoon the same day.

Getting wind that Arnold had summoned the camp's constable, Joe burst into the bank (and store), to startle one E.H. Tracy as he was taking down a sign above the counter.

SIMPSON: "Hello, Tracy, what are you doing here?"
TRACY: "Holding up the bank. *(A wan attempt at humor.)* Hah, hah."
SIMPSON: *(Turning to Jim Arnold, nearby.)* "Jim, what have you got against me?"
ARNOLD: "Joe, I have nothing against you, but when under the influence of liquor you are intensely ugly."
SIMPSON: *(Drawing his gun.)* "By God, your time has come! *(Takes two steps back)* You've got to die." *(Levels his gun, shoots Arnold.)*
ARNOLD: *(Falling to the floor mortally wounded.)* "For Christ's sake, don't shoot me again. *(Agonizing pause.)* You've got me now."

It was at this point that, hearing the shot, Constable Henry Sellers was on the scene. He was unarmed.

SIMPSON: *(With gun in hand)* "Do you want anything?"

The Constable shook his head, fled.

Act II

Minutes later.

Accompanied by Gordon McBain, a boozy lowlife crony, Simpson exited the bank and, crossing the street, street strode into Jack Shehey's restaurant for a bite to eat. He felt the killing justified.

SIMPSON: (Boasting) "I'm a Bohemian, a hero, and true blue!"

Meanwhile, Constable Sellers had gotten his hands on a shotgun, tried to load it, jammed it, then settled for a revolver. In a fit of bravery, he rushed to the restaurant, to grasp Simpson's gun hand by the wrist. He grappled as well with Joe's pal Gordon.

SELLERS: (To Gordon) "If you don't get away, I'll kill you!"

Joe Simpson squirmed, seeking to shoot Sellers in the stomach. He fired three shots—into the floor. Ben Epstein now entered the fray, and managed to wrest Simpson's gun from his hand as the constable slammed him face down onto the floor.

One Fred Oaks was next on the scene, and proceeded to excoriate Joe Simpson for the awful thing he'd done.

SIMPSON: "Yes Fred, and I had a lot of fun doing it. Just look at the fun I had doing it!"
OAKS: "Joe, the man can't get well."
SIMPSON: "And I am glad of it! Glad of it!" (He would maniacally repeat this a half dozen times.)

Two hours later, across the way in his Skidoo Trading Company's store, Jim Arnold died.

Meanwhile, Constable Sellers had jailed Joe Simpson, pestered at one point by Simpson's crony Gordon McBain, wondering if he couldn't buy Joe a drink or two.

Act III

Early morning, three days later.

On their way to work, Ben Epstein and two companions spied "something hanging to a telephone post. Found it to be the body

SKIDOO NEWS.

VOL. II, NO 18   SKIDOO, INYO COUNTY, CALIFORNIA, SATURDAY, APRIL 25, 1908   TEN CENTS

MURDER IN CAMP
Murderer Lynched
WITH GENERAL APPROVAL

of Joe Simpson. It had a rope around its neck." They had no idea—no idea at all—how the body got up there.

Simpson's body was cut down and dumped into a mine shaft, only to be retrieved the next day and rehung for the benefit of a *Los Angeles Herald* photographer dispatched to the camp.

The lynching, the Skidoo News declared, was:

> . . . JUST, CHEAP, and SALUTORY in the lesson it conveys. Would-be badmen, as they bowl along the road on their triumphal entry of Skidoo, will note the number, the stoutness, and great convenience of the telephone poles, and reflect thereon.

Goodbye, Skidoo. Until the camp gave up the ghost a year after the murder and hanging, a stage connected highland Skidoo with alkali flat Ballarat.

Wood was scarce, but not mud. Ballarat construction was mostly adobe, with roofs and walls subject to sudden collapse.

On down the Panamints, at the edge of an alkali flat. What remains of Ballarat.

A room at Ma Callaway's Hotel (left) cost a prospector 50 cents. Around the corner, Tom Biggin's "Corral & Burro Emporium" looked after his faithful companions. Chris Wicht's Headquarters Saloon is on down the street and to the right.

Dating to the late 1890s, Ballarat had a peak population of 250—that in the wake of the Wall Street Panic of '07, sagged to 40. Poet-prospector Clarence Eddy recalled, "When I first hove in sight of Ballarat I thought 'What a hell of a place this is. Nothing to do, and nobody to hum.'" But, after few days and nights, he had a change of heart. To his liking, the resident Desert Rats were colorful company, *doves du priarie* responded to a tip of the hat, and the place was cheerfully godless. Ballarat never had a church.

With nearby mining shut down, Ballarat was essentially a supply camp—and haven—for prospectors needful of powder, square meals, and drink.

In Ballarat, the Dutchman Chris Wicht's Headquarters Saloon offered a man a respite from the burning sun, the opportunity to peddle a sack of high grade, and "heavy wassail." Poet-prospector Eddy delighted in "a continual merry click of glasses, the fragrant odor of good Havanas, the effervescence of Champagne, and the familiar $$$ sound of poker chips, faro and rouletted wheels, as the games started up, to give a full accompaniment for the evening's entertainment."

A touring car has made it to the camp, and a young woman has donned a chauffeur's cap. Why are the men pointing at her? Is she local or in from the big city? Of good or bad repute?

149

An informal Chris Wicht. Tending bar, he customarily wore a forked tail coat, vest, celluloid collar, string tie, and derby hat—a figure of a fading West.

A quiet afternoon in Chris Wicht's celebrated saloon. (This rare interior likely dates to the camp's decline.)

Here, the local Montana Kid might serenade patrons with his home-made fiddle, and entertainment was to be had in tales of Death Valley life: Talk of petrified monkey eyes, electrical rattlesnakes, and the magnetic ledge that wouldn't let go of Jim Farley's mule, inopportunely shot with iron shoes. The ledge seized up Jim as well, or rather his hobnailed boots. And it was a long walk to camp in his stocking feet. The incident explained—somehow—why Farley had crazy spells between the full and new moon.

When times were tough, food and drink were on the house. Chris did this because "I couldn't help but feel I owed them something. They always left their dollars with me when they had 'em." If prospectors wished, they could sleep on the floor or on the sole pool table between Rhyolite, Nevada, and Independence, California.

Shorty Harris *(center)* poses with a party passing through. He was ever in a hurry, a friend said, "to stay in front of the slow wagon wheel of death."

Between 1908 and 1915, one by one, Ballarat's old timers moved on.

In the end, there was a hotel where no one checked in or out, and a post office where mail was never sent or arrived. Chris Wicht padlocked his saloon when he was down to jumpy, garrulous Shorty Harris as his one steady customer.

In the end, over 20,000 claims had staked and recorded in Death Valley. And for all that, there were a hundred or so marginal diggings, and no more than a half-dozen rich, profitable mines.

In the end, Shorty Harris, holed up in Ballarat's derelict schoolhouse, had the camp to himself. And he had no regrets for his rags-to-riches-and-back-again round of life. "Who the hell wants $10,000,000?" he'd ask. "It's the game, man—the game."

When, penniless, Shorty died, well-wishers honored his wish that he be carted over the Panamints and buried at the edge of Death Valley's salt flats. With the expectation that the short man would arrive in a child's coffin, a grave was dug. Instead, a wagon delivered a full-sized box. With the weather rank and his admirers anxious to move on, he was interred standing up.

Any sermonizing was forestalled by "Why don't they plant him? Why don't they plant the old sonofabitch?"

Shorty received a three-word oration: "Dust to dust."

It could well be an epitaph for an era.

Shorty and fellow-prospector Jim Sherlock.

A howling, spiraling wind—a "sand augur" or "dust devil"—is paid little heed. But if there was the slightest flame to be fanned, all hell could break loose. A cigar lit after lunch could ignite a camp, and by dinnertime, render it ashes. *(Right)*: Of the Mojave's larger camps, only Rhyolite was spared a holocaust. With no horses to be wrangled or tacked, a man-powered pumper could be on the scene in minutes. Note the building in the background, a doctor's office constructed not of wood, but of fireproof adobe.

Visited by the Angel of Fire

With dread certainty, the Angel would visit a camp, and take wing for the next.[14] Hundred foot wide streets lessened the destruction, but not by much. Wood was tinder dry and water hard come by. Add to this stoves and lamps fueled by coal, oil, and gasoline. And, ever a factor, there was the "Mojave zephyr," described as "anything but a gentle zephyr, yet by using both hands any person of ordinary strength could keep their hat on."

Given a rare windless day, a fire could create its own devastating sirocco.

In January of 1898 the Angel was abroad in Randsburg, with a return visit five months later. On both occasions, the only way to forestall complete ruination was to stand back as a "powder brigade" dynamited building after building in the fire's path.

With the demolition of a hardware store, "there was a regular kitchen shower of everything from dishes, pots, and pans to wash tubs and chamber pots." In the direction

14. The name bespoke vengeance. When in Greenwater the office of the *Death Valley Chuck-Walla* burned to the ground, the *Las Vegas Age* credited poetic justice: "The *Chuck-Walla* was roasted alive by the Angel of Fire because of the many unholy things it has printed."

Randsburg, 1898. "The flames and smoke, mounted hundreds of feet skyward, made a grand but awful sight." (*Los Angeles Times*, the next morning)

Randsburg's Methodist Church consumed by the Angel, vilified as well as the "Red-tongued demon of Rand Mountain."

of Fiddler's Gulch, firefighters "pinned their hopes on the fluzy barn. Being partly covered with corrugated iron sheeting, they thought it might stop the fire. But when the flames licked their way up its side the whole building suddenly burst skyward, and the girls barely escaped with their lives, through windows as well as doors."

This was the recollection of young Marcia Wynn, who recalled a "poor little redlight thing. Shivering in her skimpy wrapper, the only thing she had on, she turned forlornly to Grandmother. 'Oh! I don't know what I'm going to do for the cold. I ain't got no more clothes 'n a jackrabbit!'"

Destined to be chronically ablaze, Goldfield had the benefit of a large and enthusiastic volunteer Fire Department headed by no-nonsense Chief Claude Inman (also Chief Constable). The only casualty of the camp's first major fire was a parrot rescued from the advancing flames—that winged back to its empty cage, its last testament the cry of "Fire! Fire. . . ."

As well as a shift in the wind at a critical moment, sloshed kegs of beer were credited in saving the day.

Early on, water was in short supply. But, in time, pipelines would be laid that would assure Goldfield a minimum of 400,000 gallons a day. Not only that, limestone—believed to be fireproof—was now quarried for the construction of banks, mercantiles, schools, and office blocks. For, as the *Goldfield Review* foretold, "there is no telling when the next visitation will occur."

Tonopah, 1908. Photographer E.W. Smith was to record a saloon's crumble to embers (and then enhance his images with red dye). This was the first of a year of devastating fires fought, if fought at all, by a woefully inadequate volunteer fire department. In time, the better part of the town's Redlight district would be incinerated, including Julius Goldsmith's renowned Big Casino dance hall.

Goldfield, 1905. "On Saturday last the fire fiend got in his terrible work. The long-looked-for burning of the town almost happened. As it was, two blocks of business houses were burned to the ground and now lie a heaping mass of ruins." *(Goldfield Review)*

For several years, visitations by the Angel of Fire were confined to single structures, including two newly-built hotels.

But then, late on a Saturday night in 1911, two mill men up at Goldfield's Florence Mine took a break at their work station. As they unlatched their dinner pails, they looked one to the other. Was it a whiff of smoke they smelled? Opening the door to the adjoining boiler room, they discovered its woodwork ablaze. They "blew the big whistle."[15]

Firefighters, quickly on the scene, connected their hoses—only to have the mill's water pressure dribble and die. All they could do was, dumbfounded, watch the fire burn on, "which was one of the most spectacular imaginable."

The horror of it all was that, with flames now licking the Florence's gallows frame, the mine's night shift was still underground.

It was then that cage tender Dick Egan rose to the occasion. Like Tonopah's legendary Big Bill, he threw caution to the fiery winds, and coolly and methodically saw to it that every last miner was brought to the surface.

15. This and quotes to follow from the *Goldfield Tribune*, December 4, 1911.

NIGHT PHOTO
BURNING OF FLORENCE-GOLDFIELD MILL
DEC. 2ᵈ

Wallpaper in a miner's shack attests to a quick response by chief Inman and his crew.

Dawn, July 6. Guests at the Goldfield Hotel were stunned by what they witnessed across the street. Regrettably, no one alerted the fire station, two blocks away.

Walking clear of the destruction, he turned to witness "a blast furnace with everything about the collar of the shaft at white heat."

Within weeks the Florence mine's shaft was cleared and its gallows frame rebuilt. Yet, in the wake of the stock market Panic of '07, the glory that was Goldfield was to fade.

A few years and "sand and tumbleweeds blew inside the broken windows of once fine houses and birds nested in living rooms not so long ago the glittering scenes of social triumphs. The moguls were gone." The visitor who wrote this sought solace in the quarters of the Montezuma Club, once the preserve of the camp's elite, only to find it "transformed from a roaring place of joy unconfined to a gloomy retreat where one might contemplate suicide and find it attractive."

Yet Goldfield hung on, for ever-deeper underground, the gold was still there.

Then in 1910, the State of Nevada abolished gambling, and frock-coated Knights of the Green Cloth exited the camp.

In 1913, a flash flood tore through Goldfield camp, wiping out the greater part of its Redlight.

The years drifted by.

In 1921, Prohibition was to curtail the option of drowning one's sorrows in drink.

With no dice to roll or elbow to hoist, the Fourth of July of 1923 paled compared to celebrations of yore. The day's highlights, as reported in the *Goldfield Tribune*:

Little Ray Madden, Jr., 21 months old, carried his spud all the way in the potato and spoon race, and was not last either. Then Jim Murphy had an idea he could finish in front of Mrs. Connolly in the 50-yard dash. Mrs. Connolly finished a clean 10 yards in front. Mrs. Connolly is a natural athlete.

Then, two days later (in a prospector's exclamation), "hell was afloat!"

The source of the blaze—across the street from the Goldfield Hotel and next to the Brown-Parker Garage.

Here is what happened.

Across from the hotel, with Prohibition still in force, bootlegger T.C. Rhea had ninety gallons of moonshine on hand—but nevertheless, to bottle more, was up and about stoking his still.

At 6:40 a.m., it exploded.

In the Goldfield Hotel, opposite Rhea's place, Harry Ruell leapt from his bed to his window. In the street below, "Wild Bill the Swede" shouted, "Fire! Fire!" Fogged by sleep, Harry Ruel failed to report this. In fact, not a soul thought to ring up the fire department—for fifteen critical minutes.

In that fateful interval, the fire spread to the Brown-Parker Garage, there to detonate fifty pounds of dynamite packed in a prospector's motor car—hurling a fragment of red-hot metal through a Goldfield Hotel third floor window, into the bed of a startled but unscathed W.J. Tobin.

The blast shattered the hotel's showcase plate glass windows. Guests fled. Yet, constructed of brick and granite, the grand structure would survive.

Once notified, firemen were quickly on the scene, but try as they might—even dynamiting buildings in the fire's path—there was no stopping the holocaust, no appeasing the Angel's rage. Sparks rode a fifty-mile-an-hour wind. "Shacks and massive stone buildings crumbled as though of wax. . . . The National Hotel presented an almost unbroken firewall. The building melted like silver before a blowpipe, in less than fifteen minutes tumbling into the basement."[16] By 3:00 p.m.—when the fire burned itself out—a hundred and fifty families were homeless, and half the camp—including some twenty-five commercial blocks—was leveled.

16. *Tonopah Daily Times*, July 7, 1923.

A block north of Crook Street, between Main and Fifth. Note the smoldering arch.

The arch today: All that was left of the Sideboard Saloon.

IXON BLDG·T·G·R·R·OFFICE BLDG

July 7, 1923. To the left: the remains of mogul George Nixon's office block. To the right: the offices of the Tonopah & Goldfield Railroad. The choice of "fireproof" local limestone was unfortunate. The fire evaporated moisture trapped in the stone—exploding it, rendering it dust.

There would be no rebuilding, no recovery. Within weeks, a third of all Goldfielders would move on. Yet, Goldfield would not, and has not given up the ghost. Generations of kids would play hide-and-seek in the cellar holes of once bustling and riotous establishments. The camp would remain the seat of Esmeralda County, even as over the years, the population—once as high as 24,000—dwindled to today's few hundred.

Even so, old timers will swear that when the wind blows just so, there is gold flour in the air—and that a half dozen miles from the camp, there is an buried extension of Goldfield's celebrated lode, severed by a fault.

"Yup, there's been an outfit diamond drilling out there," confided a Goldfield friend, "and coring highgrade samples. So they say. Got some local folks accumulating real estate for the rush, if there is a rush."

"The ore. How deep?"

"Word is they've been drilling and drilling, and have yet to hit bottom. Could be worth billions."

"Or nothing?"

"Nothing? Could be, could just be. Bar talk and smoke. Wouldn't be the first time."

To the north and west, the carnage from a balcony of the Goldfield Hotel.

Mirage at Silver Dry Lake, north of Baker, California.

Gas station and dance hall (with cribs out back), Darwin, California.

Epilogue

A Hidden and Forsaken World

A preserved miner's shack on the grounds of Tonopah's Central Nevada Museum.

Derelict camps are scattered like dice across the Mojave. Some have sparks of life, some are ghosts, many are no more than patches of rusted cans and broken glass.

But consider this: Beneath these remnants, beneath the desert's shimmering heat waves and mirages, there lies a haunting, hidden and forsaken world. Of thousands of miles of tunnels—adits, drifts, raises, and winzes. Of enormous gouged-out stopes.

It is a world no longer echoing with explosions. Gone are rattling ore cars, the ring of signal bells, the whir of descending and ascending cages. But it's not a silent world. Water drips, rotting timbers creak. Every so often—unable to withstand elemental pressure of untold tons of rock—a wall caves, a roof collapses.

Closer to the surface, doves and rattlesnakes seek refuge in broken-laddered shafts.

The abandonment was gradual. As Eastern capital pulled its investments, mines were opened to leasers, then their kin, "pocket miners." With luck, they would hole into ore the original owners had overlooked. That failing, they'd risk their lives taking out pillars still glistening with gold or silver.

At the far end of the glory hole, diverging drifts seek—and block out—the ore's extent.

A cavernous glory hole. A mine owner's dream; back-breaking work for a miner.

On these pages there's an evocation of this hidden world. The photographer is unknown. What is certain is that in the camp he took great care in selecting his angle, and then with magnesium powder, lighting the 800-foot level of the Bagdad mine, the richest in the southern Mojave.

From the end of World War I to the present, city dwellers—who once shunned the desert—were now to seek and appreciate its solitude and peace. Parks and preserves were created. The focus shifted from what might lay underground to the wilderness above, with its amazingly adapted plants, its unique wildlife, its scenic wonders.

Get-rich-quick schemes and dreams gave way to quiet curiosity and the attraction of a natural world, however harsh. Adventuress Edna Brush Perkins, in her 1922 *White Heart of the Mojave*, was to portray Death Valley as . . .

. . . wild and fearful and wonderful. A young moon, sharp as a curved knife blade, hung over the hills. We went out into the vague brightness among the ghostly bushes, and at last onto the darkness of the lake-bed . . .

We walked on and on, full of a strange terrible happiness . . .

We stood still listening to the silence. It was immense and all enveloping . . .

Such a palace of dreams.

There would be no more excitements.

The prospector as quaint artifact. A scrapbook's caption records a tourist posing "beside an honest, good old pioneer 89 year gold miner at his shanty he is dead broke but is good harted [*sic*] and cheerful."

No79. Oliver M. Morris beside an honest, good old pioneer 89 year gold miner at his shanty he is dead broke but is good harted and cheerful.

Times had changed. Farewell frock coats and floral hats. Farewell Old West.

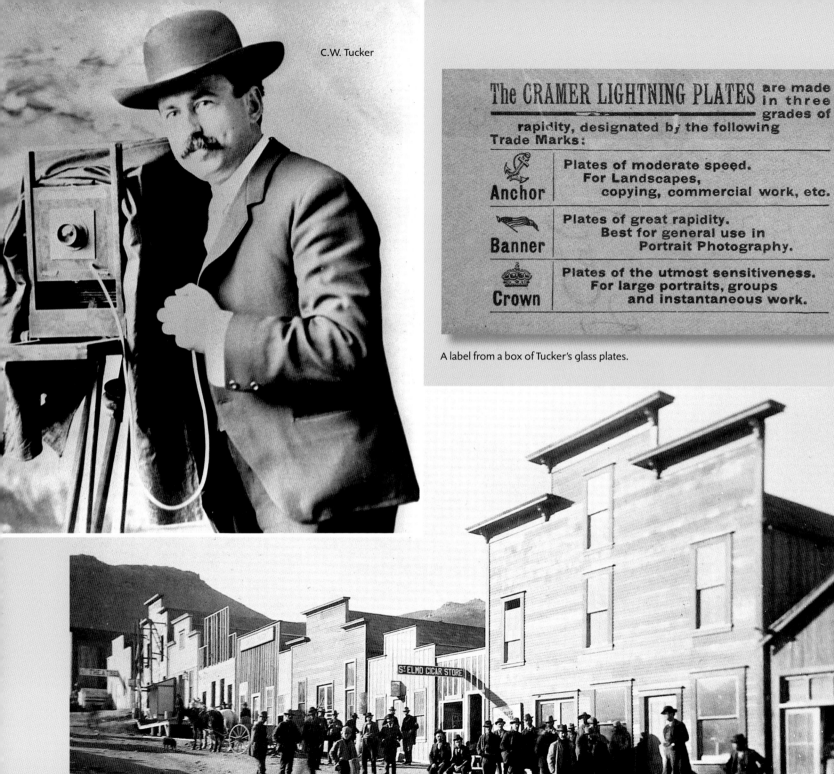

C.W. Tucker

The CRAMER LIGHTNING PLATES are made in three grades of rapidity, designated by the following Trade Marks:

Anchor	Plates of moderate speed. For Landscapes, copying, commercial work, etc.
Banner	Plates of great rapidity. Best for general use in Portrait Photography.
Crown	Plates of the utmost sensitiveness. For large portraits, groups and instantaneous work.

A label from a box of Tucker's glass plates.

St ELMO CIGAR STORE

Frozen in silver: Randsburg, 1896

Appendix A:

Photographers of the Mojave

Prior to 1890, frontier photography was an awkward, painstaking, lonely enterprise. In a horse–drawn, cramped darkroom, glass plates were coated with syrupy albumen or collodian as a matrix for silver nitrate. Exposures were hit or miss, and often required several seconds, with the man behind the camera praying nothing would move. He then would develop and fix his images on the spot.

As a wave of strikes were made in the Mojave, that was to change. George Eastman, founder of Kodak, introduced his "American film," a flexible, dry paper film that could be wound in a 24 exposure roll, and could be developed days or even months later. Advances in cameras followed. Saunderson's "hand and stand" could be freed of a tripod and hand–held. A combination of fast lenses and sensitive emulsions cut exposure times to an amazing 1/60th of a second. No longer was it necessary to ask a subject to stiffly pose; action could be frozen.

Mojave photographers were quick to explore a realm of possibilities. A dark, stormy sky wasn't a problem for Randsburg's Charles W. Tucker (p. 16). Forsaking magnesium flash powder, Goldfield's Arthur Allen shot naturally–lit, evocative interiors of the camp's eateries and saloons (p. 79). Rhyolite's C. J. Back was able to venture—on foot with his Poco camera—to the remote reaches of Death Valley and return with one–of–a–kind images of Marble Canyon and Emigrant Springs (pp. 129 & 141). Rhyolite's A.E. Holt and Goldfield's Larson captured

FIRST FLOOR
PALM STUDIO & STATIONERY
HOUSE
GOLDFIELD NEV.
P E LARSON
PROP

To make ends meet, desert photographers prospected, wrote newspaper pieces, speculated in mining stock, and sold real estate. Goldfielder Per Larson opened a stationery and gift shop. With someone else squeezing the bulb, he's to be found over by the pipes and stuffed rabbits. Behind him, in a nook that doubled as a portrait studio, a customer samples a mandolin. An immigrant Swede, Per was a droll fellow. Note the above caption's "First Floor." There was no second floor.

the desert's sweep and the sprawl of its booming camps with extraordinary 180–degree panoramic images (pp 110–111 & 118–119).

Amateurs, too, would have their role. As little as 85 cents had a "take–u–quick" in a mail from Sears Roebuck. Folding models with superior astigmatic lenses were affordable. Trying out her new camera, Mimosa Pittman was astounded by her accidental capture of a Tonopah lightning strike (p. 33). And many a "photographer unknown" is to be thanked for rare—sometimes only—images of ephemeral Death Valley camps.

And all the while, Tonopah's E.W. Smith was to stick with a pre–1880 wet plate process—proof that it is a photographer's feeling for humanity, discerning eye, and sense of a magic moment that sets him apart (see his portraits, pp. 38–47).

Ideal for desert vistas, a clockwork–driven, rotating Cirkut camera exposed negatives five feet long.

E.W. Smith and his loyal Shep.

Faro in a saloon along the Colorado River.

Appendix B:

Faro and "Bucking the Tiger"

Early Faro cards were believed to have images of tigers on their backs, leading to the notion that playing the generally crooked game was tantamount to sharing a cage with a hungry big cat. You "bucked the Tiger."

Here's how Faro was played.

A standard fifty–two card deck was shuffled and placed face–up in a spring–loaded dealing box. Bets were then placed of a thirteen card layout—ace through king—glued to a felt–covered board. In Faro, whether a card was a spade or diamond was inconsequential; numbers only—of whatever suit—were what mattered.

Discarding a top *soda card*, the dealer then slid out cards in pairs—or *turns*: first a *losing card* and then a *winning card*. Say you placed your chips on the layout's seven. If the losing card was a seven, your chips went to the house. But then, if the winning card was a seven, your bet was doubled. So it went, with subtleties and variations, down through the deck. A dealer's slight advantage—2 percent at most—was gained when, in a turn, the winning and losing cards bore the same number, and whatever was at stake went to the house.

Faro talk survives in terms like *keeping tabs* and *going in hock*. Players were *punters*. A punter might be a *piker*. The game was fast–paced, suspenseful, and seemingly above–board. In fact, for all to see, a dealer's assistant—a *coffin driver*—kept tabs on the cards played with an abacus–like *case counter* (or *coffin*). If there was a crowd and the game was heated, a helpful *lookout* to the dealer's right would advise punters in the event they lost track of their bets.

With a case counter to the left, Faro's fateful layout.

Now for the truth of the matter.

Even if the play was innocent, punters were at a psychological disadvantage. From their vantage point, the cards were upside–down (facing the dealer), and they bore no numerals, only spots, difficult to distinguish if a player was inebriated.

Add now, the wiles of a crooked dealer. His tin dealing box was often fitted with intricate, hidden mechanisms alerting him to upcoming shaved, sanded, or pin–pricked cards that could be held back or double–dealt.

And a truly accomplished card sharp could execute a "Faro shuffle" that would pair as many as four like–numbered cards, and increase the house's odds by up to 25 percent. Hugh Maskelyne, an 1890s English pasteboard wizard, was knowledgeable as to Western Faro knavery. His conclusion:

> "This Faro is a hard–hearted monarch whose constant delight is the slaughter of innocents. Faro's victims can hardly hope for succor from a daughter of Faro, for his only two offspring are greed and fraud. Those who bow the head and bend the knee to Faro are simply ministering to these two, his children."[17]

17. Honest play, overseen by the State of Nevada, was a death knell for Faro. Dealer intensive and with a slim margin for the house, the game faded and folded. The game was last played in Nevada casinos in the 1930s.

Chronology of the Mojave's Early 20th Century Mining Camps

Population: Less than 100   100–1000   1000–5000   5000–10,000   Over 20,000

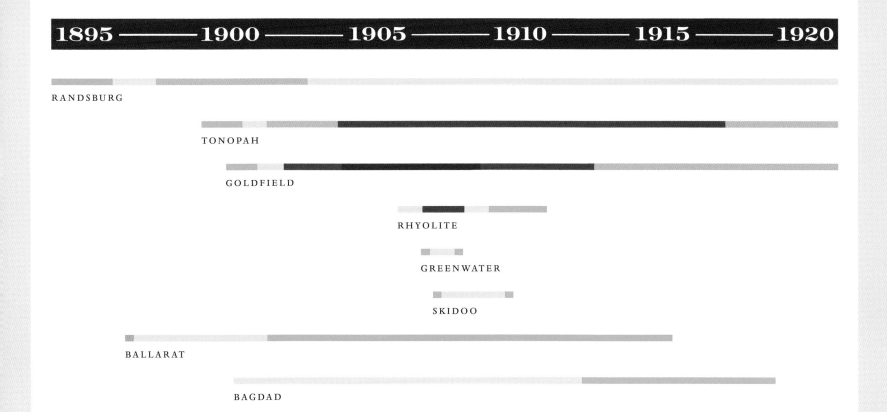

1895 — 1900 — 1905 — 1910 — 1915 — 1920

RANDSBURG

TONOPAH

GOLDFIELD

RHYOLITE

GREENWATER

SKIDOO

BALLARAT

BAGDAD

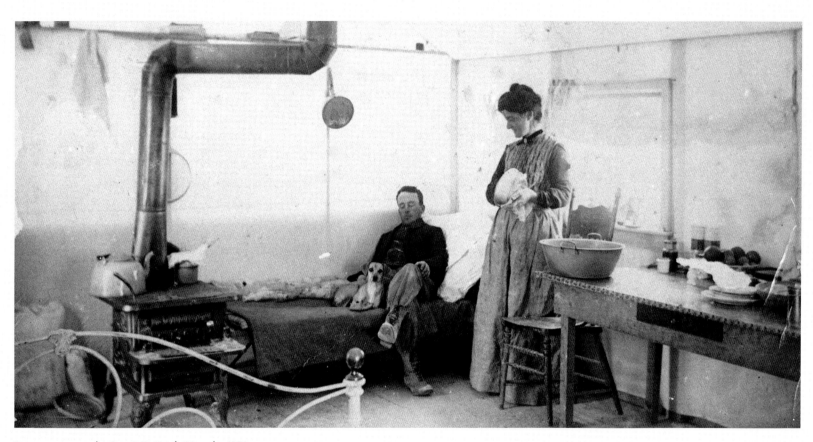

For many, as good as it got. Tonopah, Nevada, 1904.

Photography Credits

The Mojave is rife with illusion. What actually happened, what was real? What was a fantasy, a mirage? The desert's photographs shared this uncertainty. Often, it is unclear who a photographer was, or just where an image was taken. (In one instance, this author found duplicate prints of the same image labeled "Goldfield," "By Colorado River," and "Tombstone.")

I have done my best to sort this out, and duly apologize for any (near inevitable) misattribution. Beyond this, I am deeply and gratefully indebted to the book's sources. They ranged from a sheriff's shoebox to a sack of 1895 glass plates abandoned in a mine tunnel to the climate-controlled holdings of great libraries.

Multiple photographs on a page are listed clockwise from upper left (a–b–c–d). If known, photographers are credited in boldface.

Not listed below: color photographs taken by the author.

Cover:	Nevada State Museum, **Per Larson**
i:	Nevada Historical Society, **Per Larson**
ii:	Huntington Library
v:	Nevada Historical Society
vi–vii:	Huntington Library
ix:	Huntington Library
2:	Huntington Library
4:	Seaver Center, Los Angeles County Museum of Natural History, **W.L. Wall**
5 a:	Huntington Library
5 b:	Nevada Historical Society
6–7:	Author's collection
8:	Norm Larcom collection
9:	Author's collection
10 a:	Marcia Rittenhouse Wynn collection
10b:	Covina Historical Society, **C.W. Tucker**
11a:	Norm Larcom collection, **C.W. Tucker**
11 b–13 a:	Covina Historical Society, **C.W. Tucker**
13 b–14:	California State Library, **Henry C. Wilson**
15:	Huntington Library
16–17:	Covina Historical Society, **C.W. Tucker**
18:	Huntington Library

19:	Nevada Historical Society
21–25:	Huntington Library
26:	Nevada Historical Society, **E.W. Smith**
27:	Nevada Historical Society
28:	Nevada Historical Society
29:	Author's collection, **E.W. Smith**
30–31 a:	Nevada Historical Society, **E.W. Smith**
31 b:	Central Nevada Historical Society, **E.W. Smith**
32:	Mrs. Hugh Brown collection, **E.W. Smith**
33:	Central Nevada Historical Society, **Mimosa Pittman**
34–36 a:	Central Nevada Historical Society, **E.W. Smith**
36 b:	Nevada Historical Society, **E.W. Smith**
37–44:	Central Nevada Historical Society, **E.W. Smith**
45 a:	Nevada Historical Society, **E.W. Smith**
45 b:	Central Nevada Historical Society, **E.W. Smith**
46 a:	Nevada Historical Society, **E.W. Smith**
46 b–47:	Central Nevada Historical Society, **E.W. Smith**
48:	Nevada Historical Society, **E.W. Smith**
50:	Nevada Historical Society
52 a:	Nevada Historical Society, **E.W. Smith**
52 b–53 a:	Author's collection
53 b:	Huntington Library
53 c:	Central Nevada Historical Society, **E.W. Smith**
54:	Nevada Historical Society
55 a–56:	Central Nevada Historical Society
57:	Nevada Historical Society
58:	Central Nevada Historical Society
61:	Huntington Library
62 a:	Bryan Smalley collection
62 b:	C.B. Glasscock collection
63–64 a:	Nevada Historical Society
64 b:	Nevada State Museum
65:	Nevada State Museum, **Per Larson**
66:	Bryan Smalley collection
67:	Nevada Historical Society, **E.W. Smith**
68:	Central Nevada Historical Society
69 a:	Nevada State Museum, **Per Larson**
69 b:	Seaver Center, Los Angeles County Museum of Natural History
70–71:	Nevada State Museum, **Per Larson**
72 a:	Library of Congress, **West Coast Art Co.**
74:	Nevada State Museum, **Per Larson**
76:	Huntington Library, **Sanborn Map Co.**
77:	Central Nevada Historical Society, **Per Larson**
78:	Central Nevada Historical Society
79 a:	Special Collections, University of Nevada, Reno, **A. Allen**
79 b–80 a:	Nevada Historical Society, **A. Allen**
80 b:	Author's collection
80 c:	Nevada Historical Society, **A. Allen**
81 a/b:	Central Nevada Historical Society
81 c:	Special Collections, University of Nevada, Reno
82:	Sewell Thomas collection
83:	Seaver Center, Los Angeles County Museum of Natural History
84:	Nevada State Museum
85:	Nevada State Museum, **Per Larson**
91 b:	Central Nevada Historical Society
93 b:	San Francisco Public Library
97:	From *Alkali Angels*, **Marilyn Newton**
98:	Nevada State Museum, **Per Larson**
99:	Huntington Library
100 a:	Nevada Historical Society
100 b:	Huntington Library
101:	County of Inyo, Eastern California Museum
102:	Author's collection
103:	Huntington Library
104 a:	Nevada State Museum
104 b:	Colorado Railroad Museum
105:	Central Nevada Historical Society
106:	Huntington Library
107:	Author's collection
108 a:	Nevada Historical Society, **A.E. Holt**
108 b:	Mrs. H.H. Heisler collection
108 d:	Huntington Library
109 a:	Nevada Historical Society, **A.E. Holt**
109 b:	Central Nevada Historical Society
109 c:	National Park Service, Death Valley National Park, **Burton Frasher**
110 a:	Nevada Historical Society, **A.E. Holt**
110 b:	A friend of the project, **David Meltzer**

113:	County of Inyo, Eastern California Museum
115 b:	Author's collection
116 b:	Author's collection
116 c:	Nevada Historical Society, **Per Larson**
117:	Nevada State Museum, **Per Larson**
118 a:	Library of Congress, **Per Larson**
120:	Author's collection
121 a:	National Park Service, Death Valley National Park, **Azariah Y. Pearl**
121 b:	Author's collection
122:	Huntington Library
123 a:	Nevada State Library, **Per Larson**
123 b:	Bryan Smalley collection
124:	Bancroft Library, University of California, Berkeley, **Dane Coolidge**
125:	Arizona Historical Foundation, **Dane Coolidge**
126:	Author's collection, **Dane Coolidge**
127:	Nevada State Museum, **Per Larson**
128 a:	National Park Service, Death Valley National Park
128 b–129 a:	National Park Service, Death Valley National Park, **C.J. Back**
129 b:	Nevada Historical Society, from *Death Valley Magazine*, 1908
130–131:	Arizona Historical Foundation, **Dane Coolidge**
132–133:	Author's collection
134:	Automobile Club of Southern California
135:	Author's collection
136:	National Park Service, Death Valley National Park, **Azariah Y. Pearl**
137 a:	Arizona Historical Foundation, **Dane Coolidge**
138 a:	National Park Service, Death Valley National Park
138 b:	California State Library, **Azariah Y. Pearl**
141 a:	National Park Service, Death Valley National Park
141 b:	National Park Service, Death Valley National Park, **C.J. Back**
142:	County of Inyo, Eastern California Museum
143 a:	National Park Service, Death Valley National Park
143 b/c:	County of Inyo, Eastern California Museum
144:	National Park Service, Death Valley National Park
145–146:	County of Inyo, Eastern California Museum

147 a:	Arizona Historical Foundation, **Dane Coolidge**
148:	County of Inyo, Eastern California Musuem
149:	Norm Larcom collection
150:	George Pipkin collection
151:	Automobile Club of Southern California
152:	Huntington Library
153:	C. Lorin Ray collection
154 a:	Covina Historical Society, **C.W. Tucker**
154 b:	Roberta Starry collection
155:	Nevada Historical Society, **E.W. Smith**
156 a:	Nevada Historical Society
156 b:	Nevada State Museum
157 a:	Nevada Historical Society
159–161:	Central Nevada Historical Society
162:	Special Collections, University of Nevada, Reno Library
166–167:	Huntington Library
168 a:	Seaver Center, Los Angeles County Museum of Natural History
168 b:	National Park Service, Death Valley National Park
169:	Nevada Historical Society
170 a/b:	Covina Historical Society
172:	Nevada State Museum, **Per Larson**
173 a:	Central Nevada Historical Society
173 b:	Author's collection
174–176:	Huntington Library
178:	Central Nevada Historical Society

Back cover
a:	Central Nevada Historical Society, **E.W. Smith**
b:	**Bonnie Clapp**
c:	Eastern Califonia Museum

Acknowledgments

A highlight of this project was the opportunity to spend some time with Mojave desert dwellers, spirited souls all. Young or old, they couldn't imagine living anywhere else. And this book wouldn't have seen the light of day without them.

In the Randsburg area, gnarly prospector Bruce Minard and his dreamy compatriot Billy Blue ruminated on the lure of their life's work. Underground, Billy Varga was living proof of the hard work and hazards of a hard rock miner.

In Tonopah, Eva LaRue and Angela Haag, stalwarts of the Central Nevada Museum, introduced me to eye–opening images taken by E.W. Smith. Further, Jim Galli gave me an idea of what it would have been like to be a panoramic photographer (he personally favors pre–1910 cameras and lenses—with impressive results). And Clair Blackburn was giving his all to keep an awareness of his town's past alive.

In Goldfield, I was enthusiastically aided by John Ekman, by Jim and Joan Price, and by irascible Deputy Sheriff Brian Smalley. "Interested in old photos? I've got a shoe box of 'em." My appreciation as well to

preservationists Jim Marsh, Dominic Pappalardo, Amanda Elsee, and "Little Bit" (Elaine Arnold), who when she wasn't pursuing local history, tended bar in the Santa Fe Saloon, Nevada's oldest continuously operated thirst parlor.

In Death Valley, ranger Linda Greene provided a wealth of historical information, and Blair Davenport, curator of the park's archives, offered access to thousands of images. The late George Pipkin was long the area's unofficial historian, and his daughter, Lit Brush, kindly lent images collected by her father.

Given to roaming the desert in search of its secrets and wonders, Norm Larcom enthusiastically supported the project, and frequently called to offer ideas and see how I was doing. I enjoyed his many and colorful stories, as I did chatting with Judy Palmer, the desert dynamo of Shoshone, California.

I'm indebted as well to city dwellers at the desert's edge. As I leafed through documents and photographs at the Huntington Library in San Marino, California, Alan Jutzi, curator of rare books, would appear

and with a "How about this!," offer a choice item I'd never have thought to look for. His colleague, Jennifer Watts, curator of photography, was key to finding many of the book's finest images. At the Nevada State Museum Carson City, Sue Ann Monteleone shared her knowledge of the work of photographer P.E. Larson, and in Reno, Lee Brumbaugh was my guide through the Nevada Historical Society's exhaustive and wonderful collection. Finally, in the unlikely locale of Covina, California, Robert Ihsen ushered my wife, Bonnie, and me into an abandoned jail cell used for storage by the local historical society. There he extracted a yellow box from a jumble of memorabilia, blew away a layer of dust, and opened it to reveal a dozen 8"x10" glass plate negatives exposed in 1895 by Randsburg's unsung C.W. Tucker, who qualifies as the first major photographer of the Mojave's last hurrah era.

My heartfelt gratitude goes to my wife, Bonnie, ever willing to bump down a dusty desert road in search of yet another forsaken mine. She was ever helpful, be it sharing the search for images or finding the precise point from which an old panorama was taken.

A number of the book's images were severely the worse–for–wear. Faded, scratched, torn. For their deft skills and restorative powers, I thank Judy Kessler, David Meltzer, and Molly Bosted.

Finally, Diana and Lowell Lindsay of Sunbelt Publications, had the interest, will, and wherewithal to make *Gold and Silver in the Mojave* a reality. Their able team included ace publications manager Debi Young, sharp-eyed copy editor Anita Palmer, map-maker Kathleen Wise, and Lydia D'moch, responsible for the book's imaginative design. They are an enthusiastic and talented lot.

Index

Nightfall, Death Valley.